HOCKEY AS A RELIGION

THE MONTREAL CANADIENS

OLIVIER BAUER

HOCKEY AS A RELIGION

THE MONTREAL CANADIENS

OLIVIER BAUER

Common Ground

First published in Champaign, Illinois in 2011
by Common Ground Publishing LLC
as part of the Sport and Society series

Copyright © Olivier Bauer 2011

All rights reserved. Apart from fair dealing for the purposes of study, research, criticism or review as permitted under the applicable copyright legislation, no part of this book may be reproduced by any process without written permission from the publisher.

Library of Congress Cataloging-in-Publication Data

Bauer, Olivier.
Hockey as a religion : the Montreal Canadians / by Olivier Bauer.
   p. cm.
ISBN 978-1-86335-930-6 (pbk : alk. paper) -- ISBN 978-1-86335-931-3 (pdf)
1. Montreal Canadiens (Hockey team). 2. Québec (Province)--Religion. 3. Québec (Province)--Religious life and customs. 4. Sports--Religious aspects. I. Title.

GV848.M6B38 2011
796.962'6409714471--dc23

2011019259

Cover image by Ranjaliva, "Fin de séries", Watercolor on paper, May 2011, 9x12 inches

Table of Contents

Foreword 1

Part I : Does the Habs Comprise a Religion?

Chapter 1: "The Games in Our Stadiums are a Meditation on What, Exactly?" [MONTHERLANT 1954: 55] 7
    a. The Christian as an Athlete 8

Chapter 2: Three Sports, Three Regions, Three Religions 11
    a. The Kingdom of God is Like a Game of Baseball... 12
    b. You shall Worship the Lord, your Sport... 14
    c. In the beginning was Hockey, and Hockey was with Canada, and Hockey was Canada... 16

Chapter 3: A Habs' Religion? Which Religion? 21
    a. Religion 22
    b. Institutional Religion 25
    c. Popular Religion 27
    d. Implicit Religion 29
    e. Civil Religion 30
    f. Quasi-Religon 32

Chapter 4: What is the Relationship between Sports and Religion? . 35
    a. Inclusivism 36
    b. Syncretism 38
    c. Dimorphism 39
    d. Exclusivism 41

Part II : Habs' Passion On the Thin Red Line between Faith and Idolatry

Chapter 5: The Habs 47
    a. Hockey's Gods 48
    b. State of Grace 49
    c. "Les avoir trempées dans l'eau bénite" 50
    d. Believing against all evidences 51

Chapter 6: Making the Habs a Religion 53
    a. The Victoria way 53
    b. The Jonathan way 55

Chapter 7: Three Dogmas of the Habs' Religion **59**
   a. Hockey's dogma: "A man, you shall be!" 60
   b. Quebec's dogma: "French, you shall speak!" 61
   c. Habs' dogma: "Through suffering, you shall win!" 63

Chapter 8: The Habs' Religion is not My Religion **65**

Chapter 9: On the Thin Red Line between Faith and Idolatry **67**
   a. God be with the Habs! 67
   b. God love the Habs! 70

Afterword **73**

Bibliography **77**

Foreword

The Habs' Religion![1] You may love it or hate it. You may be a worshipper, a believer or an atheist. You may think it is true religion, heresy or idolatry. But if you live in Montreal, you have to deal with it!

In 2007 when Jean-Marc Barreau and I decided to work on the topic of the "religion du Canadien de Montréal," we did not anticipate the impact of such a research on Quebec society. To be honest, for my part, I was not even certain such a religion really did exist. But I had to learn quickly! I learnt all together that the Habs are a religion in Montreal; that the fans are not always aware they are worshipers; that they love this idea; and that they want to understand what they believe in.

Since October 14, 2008 in a first interview in *Le Devoir* (a Quebec newspaper) [Gervais 2008], I had more than one opportunity to explain what I meant by "la religion du Canadien."

I taught one graduate class at the Faculty of Theology and the Sciences of Religion at the University of Montreal during the winter semester of 2008.

---

1. "Le Canadien" is the nickname of the "Club de hockey Canadien", the Montreal NHL Hockey team. In English it is known as "The Habs", which derives from "the Habitants", a depreciative nickname used to speak about the French Canadians. In French, the Club de hockey Canadien is also known as "Le Tricolore", "Les Glorieux" or "La Sainte Flanelle". Note that in 1909, when the club was founded "Canadien" only designated Francophone Canadians.

With Jean-Marc Barreau, we co-edited *La religion du Canadien de Montréal* (Fides, 2009) and I wrote a second book on my own: *Une théologie du Canadien de Montréal* (Bayard, 2011).

I was invited to scientific congresses in Montréal, QC, Ottawa, ON, Buffalo, NY, San-Diego, CA, and Kolkata, India, as well as to contribute to the Intellectual Muscle Program during the Vancouver 2010 Olympic Winter Games.

I delivered papers in various places: for general audiences in Montreal, for High School students from Switzerland, for Quebec's Ethic and Religious Culture Program teachers, in a Popular University, a Literary Seminar; in personal discussion with students from Middle School, High School and Universities; in various documentaries on Habs and Habs Passion.

I gave more than 130 interviews for various medias (newspapers, magazines, radio, television) in Quebec, Canada, the United States, and in Europe.

During that time, I read a lot of comments on forums and blogs where people took position about the Habs' religion or my way of dealing with it and received many testimonies of people confessing to me why and how they were part of this religion! Now, I know for sure that the Habs' religion does exist. Some like it. Some hate it. Some believe in it. Some fight against it. But in Montreal, the Habs are a religion and scholars on Religion have to deal with it.

And that is what I did, by writting the book you are reading. It contains two different parts.

The first part – "Does The Habs Comprise a Religion?" – is the English translation of the text I published in *La religion du Canadien de Montréal* in January 2009 [Bauer 2009]. I wrote it as an introduction to the Habs religion. I begin by presenting four comments about the relation between sport and religion in four different contexts: the Christian as an athlete in Paul's letters, baseball in the United States, soccer in Europe and hockey in Canada. I continue by elaborating five different types of religion and evaluating what it would mean if the Habs' religion were part of each of these. I conclude the first part by organizing the possible relationships between sports and religions, more specifically between the Habs and the Catholic Church.

The second part – "Habs' Passion: on the Thin Red Line Between Faith and Idolatry" – is quite original. I wrote it for "The Hockey Conference" in Buffalo, NY, working with all the information and testimonies I got from people who are part of the Habs' religion. I begin by explaining why one can even talk of a Habs' religion. I continue by giving the examples of Victoria and Jonathan, two fans who have mixed Habs and religion in two opposite ways. Then, I emphasize three dogmas, or values, of the Habs' religion: the first one is a common hockey value, the second one is a common Quebec value and the third is an exclusive Habs' value. I conclude this second part by giving my opinion about this religion, explaining how the Habs could be a part of someone's faith, but how it becomes an idolatry as soon as it pretends to be a religion.

Last, but not least, I added to the book a short meditation, explaining how the Habs logo could contain a secret Christian message!

Part I

Does the Habs Comprise a Religion?[1]

---

[1] Translated in English by Eric von Zinkernagel from BAUER, O. (2009). "Le Canadien est-il une religion?" In O. Bauer, & J.-M. Barreau (eds), *La religion du Canadien de Montréal* (pp. 29-80). Montréal: Fides. In fact, my friend Eric did a lot more than translating my paper. He accurately improved it by correcting my mistakes, by clarifying my approximations, and by adding references when I just named authors.

Chapter 1
"The Games in Our Stadiums are a Meditation on What, Exactly?" [MONTHERLANT 1954: 55]

At the risk of spoiling the suspense, we should say at the outset (the reader can now either rejoice or lament) that in a strict sense, the Habs do not comprise a religion. Both fundamentally and definitionally, the team lacks a presumed and explicit reference to something ultimately transcendent – to a Divinity, whatever S/He may be. But – and this caveat is what allows us to pursue our reflection further – there is no denying the existence of the team's religiosity. In fact, the team appears to possess many attributes of a religion – perhaps not always in the sense that some ascribe to this term, but certainly in the behaviour it provokes among its followers. In Montreal at least, there is an undeniable religious fervour attached to the Habs – a fervour that only increases as the stakes in their games rise. It is a fervour that is affirmed and expressed ever more deeply once the playoffs begin, and especially when a trophy appears within reach.

To those who are a pious or intellectual mien, it may seem iconoclastic, if not inimical, to compare sports with religion. But we are scarcely the first ones to propose this analogy. Historically, there have been quite a few eminent authorities in the fields of both sports and religion who have drawn this relationship before.

"THE GAMES IN OUR STADIUMS ARE A MEDITATION ON WHAT, EXACTLY?" [MONTHERLANT 1954: 55]

a. The Christian as an Athlete

Near the beginning of the Common Era, the apostle Paul (the great theoretician of Christianity), did not hesitate to compare the Church's faithful to his society's athletes. In his letter to the Christians at Corinth that is recorded in the New Testament (and written around the year 200), he reaffirmed the value of their efforts to progress in their faith: *"Do you remember how, on a racing-track, every competitor runs, but only one wins the prize? Well, you ought to run with your minds fixed on winning the prize! Every competitor in athletic events goes into serious training. Athletes will take tremendous pains - for a fading crown of leaves. But our contest is for an eternal crown that will never fade. I run the race then with determination. I am no shadow-boxer, I really fight! I am my body's sternest master, for fear that when I have preached to others I should myself be disqualified."* [I Corinthians 9: 24-27][1]

The comparison here is significant. The aim of the Christian life is to win the prize, a prize that will endure longer than the fading crown of leaves won by the victorious athlete. And the stakes are high. Elimination from competition threatens those who lack faith; for they will not be able to run, or box, or more importantly, even play, in Paradise. And it justifies the strenuous training they must undergo, and that Paul commends to them – an ascetic discipline even more rigorous than that required of athletes.

In other New Testament letters, an anonymous author, who nevertheless claims to speak in the name of Paul, proposes sporting metaphors as well. In his First Letter to a certain Timothy, he offers this young man (who may be athletic, though we otherwise know very little about him) the following sage advice: *"Take time and trouble to keep yourself spiritually fit. Bodily fitness has a certain value, but spiritual fitness is essential both for this present life and for the life to come"*. [I Timothy 4: 7b-8]

While conceding a value to sports, this apostle nevertheless maintains the priorities of his faith. Godliness comes first, and only then does physical exercise gain significance; while justification follows logically. Physical exercise is worthwhile only in this life; because toned muscles are of no use in the Kingdom of God. In short, disciplines of the spirit are necessary both in this life, and in the life to come. *"Fight the worthwhile battle of the faith, keep your grip on that life eternal to which you have been called, and to which you boldly professed your loyalty before many witnesses."* [I Timothy 6: 12] That is his vocation. It remains for him to achieve, if he is to justify the hopes that have been placed on him.

In his second letter to Timothy, this same author proceeds further with his allusions to sports, while making reference to the military life – perhaps the most extreme sport: *"So, my son, be strong in the grace that Jesus Christ gives. Everything that you have heard me preach in public you should in turn entrust to*

---

1. This and the following biblical quotations have been rendered from *The New Testament in Modern English* (revised edition, 1972), by J.B. Phillip.

reliable men, who will be able to pass it on to others. Put up with your share of hardship as a loyal soldier in Christ's army. Remember: 1) That no soldier on active service gets himself entangled in business, or he will not please his commanding officer. 2) A man who enters an athletic contest wins no prize unless he keeps the rules laid down." [II Timothy 2: 1-5]

It is obviously wrong here to assume that an athlete can take the prize if he has not respected the rules of the game. Yet in the stadium, as in war (from the 1st Century to the 21st), his priority should be not to lose. At the same time, the Christian life does not allow cheating – before a God who knows all, and who will reveal all, at the Last Judgment.

Anticipating that day, our author attributes to Paul the following claim: *"As for me, I feel that the last drops of my life are being poured out for God. The glorious fight that God gave me I have fought. The course that I was set I have finished, and I have kept the faith. The future for me holds the crown of righteousness which God, the true judge, will give to those who have loved what they have seen of him."* [II Timothy 4: 6-8]

As an apostle, he is satisfied with what he has accomplished. Or rather, he is an apostle who is satisfied with what God has accomplished for him – because that is what he affirms. Thanks to God, he has won, without having had to fight; thanks to God, he has not needed to engage in battle with others; thanks to God, he can feel content that he did the best he could; thanks to God, he has gained victory – not over others, but over himself. He takes no glory in his success. He rejoices simply in having fulfilled his responsibility. He awaits the crown of righteousness that has been promised to him – a reward that he prefers to all medals (whether gold, silver or bronze) that he might otherwise receive. Yet far from selfishly taking pride in this honour, he rejoices in not receiving it alone. The Christian life does not crown only one victor, while leaving the others downcast and empty-handed. Rather, God rewards all who [virtuously strive to share His love, and] wait in confidence for Christ's return. It is here that effort is transformed by grace – from the rude odour of sweat, to the sweet perfume of love!

Chapter 2
Three Sports, Three Regions, Three Religions

We hope these preliminary comments may reassure those of a pious mien, at least those who are Christians, reading these pages. Yet we still have to convince the intellectually disposed, about the appropriateness of the analogy we have proposed. Sporting sceptics need to read this entire essay through, before deciding if its arguments are reasonable and sound. Yet our task should be easier with them, because they should already know that there is nothing unusual in speaking about sports and religion in the same breath. On this matter, at least, we have the benefit of a long track record.

Without claiming to be exhaustive, or even adequately representative, we wish to propose three arguments that seem emblematic. They originated with scholars in three distinct disciplines – history, anthropology and theology; from research pursued in three countries – the United States, France and Canada; and with respect to three sports – baseball, soccer, and hockey (to allow readers from any of these nations to claim their own sport). These three approaches – despite differences not only in their conceptualization, but (especially with theology) in their methodology – evince a common conviction that there is something peculiarly religious found in sports (both for good and for ill).

Very briefly, we can say that historians have shown how Christians have made sports into a tool of evangelization, that anthropologists have employed religious concepts as a heuristic tool in illuminating various aspects of sports, and that theologians have decrypted the ways in which both players and fans have made sports into a religion.

a. The Kingdom of God is Like a Game of Baseball...

In a small book with an evocative title, *The Legend of Soccer* (or Football, as Europe refers to the game), the Swiss philosopher, Georges Haldas, proposes that the Kingdom of God can be likened to a parable about soccer: *"Verily, verily, I tell you, the Kingdom of God is like a defender, who has commit a grievous fault in the goal box (at 6 meters)..."* Haldas goes on to explain: *"If the goal is scored, whether the player in question is guilty or not, he had better drop his head like one who is penitent, and mourn his sins. But if by chance, his fault is overlooked, this same player jumps for joy, higher than everyone else, in the abrupt reversal of his fate. The last shall be first, etc."* [HALDAS 1989: 93]

Various American theologians have advanced their own sports metaphors. They have reconceived the game of baseball as an activity in which the Kingdom of God can be revealed. In a recent work devoted to baseball, religion and American culture, Christopher H. Evans explains this conviction as an article of American faith, while assessing its relevance [EVANS AND HERZOG II 2002]. He notes that at the turn of the 20th Century in the United States, the expression *"the Kingdom of Baseball"* began to circulate among liberal Protestants, modelled on their prevailing notions about the Kingdom of God. Its analogy reveals the religious value they attributed to this national pastime; but it reveals more than this, for it gives flesh to an idea that was otherwise abstract – the Kingdom of God. It may be useful then to understand how these theologians conceived this idea, a hundred years ago.

Evans highlights three features which both Kingdoms of God and Baseball appeared to share:

- First, they esteemed the values of rural and pastoral life, which must be *"reclaimed and Christianized"* – that is to say, *"cleaned up"* and *"sweetened"* – in America's cities. Thus baseball stadiums were designed as building blocks of permanent green space at the heart of the nation's urban areas.

- Second, they drew together model Christians – people filled with a joyous 'zeal for God' [Rm. 10. 2], 'labourers for the harvest' [Mt. 9: 37-38], who also knew how to rest and relax in wholesome ways. Like Christy Mathewson, (the third most victorious player in the history of baseball, and nicknamed *"The Christian Gentleman"*),[1] they possessed a proper un-

---

[1]. Christy "Matty" Mathewson (1880-1925) played mostly for the New York Giants. He achieved 373 victories throughout his career. McKim, D. K. (2002). "'Matty' and 'Ol' Pete: Divergent American Heroes," in *The Faith of 50 Million: Baseball, Religion, and American Culture*. Christopher H. Evans and William R. Herzog II (eds). Louisville, Westminster John Knox Press, 51-81.

derstanding, a robust physique, a firm conviction in their faith, a spirit of competition, and a desire to win.

- Third, the two Kingdoms were presumed to be democratically organized. Anticipating in part now what will they believed would be completely true hereafter, the Kingdom of Baseball showed *"how Americans from different social classes and ethnic groups* [could] *work together to build a better society, inspired by a common vision of the Kingdom of God"* [EVANS 2002b: 40].

Early 20th Century American Protestant and liberal theologians were fundamentally convinced that, under the following three aspects, baseball not only offered a foretaste of the Kingdom of God, but served to occasion it. They affirmed: (a) a certainty that their nation was blessed by God, (b) a hope that God would transform the nation's social relations, and (c) a conviction that they were responsible for transmitting the Gospel in order to advance the [developed] Western world (a characteristically WASP – that is to say, White, Anglo-Saxon and Protestant – belief). For them, the task of evangelization consisted in remaking the world in their image, that is to say, "*Americanizing*" it. From this perspective, it is not surprising that baseball (as one of the nation's most prized cultural possessions) came to be viewed as an activity where the Kingdom of God immediately implicated America.

But as Evans notes, three counter-arguments can be raised against this idyllic notion. First, rather than embracing all of humanity, the Kingdom of Baseball excluded many in society. It did not embrace women or African-Americans, but accommodated only white men. Second, the Kingdom of Baseball was unable to elude the ills of American society; it witnessed the greed of both owners and players, no less than the vices of cheating, racism, and doping. Finally, the Kingdom of Baseball failed to "*reclaim*" America's inner cities, from which it was finally expelled.

Although some traces of its idyllic world still persist – especially in the green spaces that its stadiums continue to protect, and in the persistence of its ideas [about heroism and redemption] that continue to be prized in popular culture – the Kingdom of Baseball has become *"a metaphorical relic of an America that no longer exists"* [Evans 2002b: 43], where the game was once the symbol of a shared national hope.

Evans goes even further in his criticism of this concept. He asserts that the Kingdom of Baseball never assumed the true proportions of an eschatological reality with which Christianity was called to deal. Historically, the classical theological debates about the Kingdom of God centered on whether it would be achieved gradually as the logical culmination of humanity's ongoing progress, or through some radical inbreaking of the Divine that entailed both redemptive and transformative suffering. Liberal American Protestantism at the beginning of the 20th Century privileged the former view while ignoring the latter. Filled with optimism and confidence in the ability of mankind, it failed to take note of the disparities between men and women, race and class, and the myriad social and cultural fractures that existed, while presuming that any apparent differences among citizens would eventually disappear in the great American melting pot. This, of course, was an illusion. As Evans points out, *"a sport that can generate feelings of rural contentment, social harmony and love can also generate resentment, anger and even destruction."* [EVANS 2002b: 45-46].

b. You shall Worship the Lord, your Sport...

Three French anthropologists (Christian Bromberger, Alain Hayot and Jean-Marc Mariottini) have recently taken a different tack in their comparison of religion and sports. In a field study on the social functions of soccer (or again, *"football"*) in Turin and Marseille, they assessed the potential for interpreting a soccer match through the lens of religion.

Against the backdrop of Latin Catholicism, the authors observed that soccer matches in Turin take place in *"an atmosphere of intense religiosity... [and can involve] prayers, the sprinkling of propitiatory salt* [by spectators] *behind the goals of the team that they support, and sometimes even their sacrifice of a cock before the game"* [BROMBERGER, HAYOT & AL. 1987: 13]. Yet that is not all. Beyond these outward manifestations, the similarities between soccer and religion can be more profound, producing striking parallels and significant isomorphisms. The entire structure of the match, the authors claimed, can be understood as a kind of religious ritual, whose relevant features could be classified. These included: *"designated officiants and their acolytes, a sequence of codified actions, a well-defined spatio-temporal frame, the expression of emotions through set means, etc."* [BROMBERGER, HAYOT & AL. 1987: 40]. The officiants or the acolytes assemble the faithful *"whose energy and excitement are expressed through strictly codified ... and vocal gestures"*, while the officiants are *"charged with executing the sacrifice, by which the faithful 'commune'"*. This takes place in *"an enclosed space dedicated to the 'cult'"*, with a sanctuary at its centre – the grass field that is *"off-limits to anyone other than the 'officiants'* [and the players]*"*. Both await the promise of sacrifice in *"the victory of the good over the bad".* The game is a contest of good over evil, of *"us"* against *"them"*, whose outcome is constantly threatened by forces of adversity and malevolence – including those of *"the referee, the wind, the rain which makes the grass slick, and officiants who lack fervour and conviction"* [BROMBERGER, HAYOT & AL. 1987: 36]. Beyond this, there are the clubs, which are *"rigorously hierarchical, modelled after the ecclesiastical system".* There are *"laws which are universally valid – the XVII Laws of the Game, to which we even refer with capital letters".* There are even *"differentiated mechanisms by which the players are idolized... which appear similar to the social, regional and professional distinctions to be found in the cult of the Saints".* There is also the language used, which distinguishes the initiated from the heathen. Moreover, there are fetishistic behaviours on the parts of both the players and their supporters – concerning their choice of clothing, their manner of dress, and their assignments in the locker room in the stadium – *"all of which elevate forms of personal and institutional magic that has been borrowed from the official religion, in order to tame and subdue the randomness of fate"* [BROMBERGER, HAYOT & AL. 1987: 35-36].

As an intellectual tour-de-force, the authors' demonstration appears largely successful. *"The analogy between a soccer match and a religious rite, defined according to an ethnology of the Beyond, and implying a rupture with the mundane world,* [as well as the existence of] *coded and repetitive behaviours, thick symbolism,* [and] *multiple beliefs – seems amply grounded, so that the category of religious ritual naturally suggests itself."* [BROMBERGER, HAYOT & AL. 1987: 40].

Yet although it *"seems amply-grounded"*, it is not – *"except as a descriptive tool that is capable of capturing behaviours, factual frameworks,* [and] *symbolic structures in a manner that is relatively comprehensive"* [BROMBERGER, HAYOT & AL. 1987: 40]. Interestingly, after pointing out the many points of commonality [that soccer and religious ritual share], the authors then proceed to offer a set of reservations [about their conceptual model], and critique the analogy that they themselves have proposed. They raise five points which threaten their description of soccer as a *"religious ritual"*:

- First, notwithstanding the existence of *"magico-religious practices, entailing a somewhat fervent, somewhat parodic affirmation of symbolic efficacy"*, there is no *"belief in the active presence of supernatural beings or forces"* in a soccer match [BROMBERGER, HAYOT & AL. 1987: 38].

- Second, unlike religious ritual, a soccer match does not rest on a *"community of intention"* which unites both officiants and participants. Certainly everyone (officiants, acolytes, players, and spectators) commune in their common quest for victory; but that is their only point of accord. For when a match takes place, there are actually *"two games with different aims and stakes occurring within the confines of a single stadium. In one, supporters from two different cities – for each of whom their team becomes a symbol of their collective identity – stand in opposition to one another. In the other, highly accomplished athletes, many of whom have moved* [over the course of their careers] *from one club to another, so that their relationship to the city in which their current club is based may be relatively minor, are engaged in competition against a closed field of fellow professionals."* [BROMBERGER, HAYOT & AL. 1987: 40].

- Third, the soccer match does not present itself as a religious ritual. Undoubtedly it includes many of the elements of ritual – it requires *"designated officiants and their acolytes, a sequence of codified actions, a well-defined spatio-temporal frame, the expression of emotions through set means"* [BROMBERGER, HAYOT & AL. 1987: 41].[2] However, it lacks an explicit religious reference that would give meaning to all of these compon-

---

2. The allusion to Turner is drawn from Turner V. W. (1972). *Les tambours d'affliction*. Paris, Gallimard; while that to Pike refers to: PIKE, K. L. (1954-1960). *Language in Relation to a Unified Theory of the Structure of Human Behavior*. Glendale, Summer Institute of Linguistics.

ents. In fact, it is only the observer who is able to attribute those meanings to what takes place. *"In other words, to recall the dichotomy that was introduced by K. L. Pike, soccer offers a ritual from an 'etic' perspective (meaning that of the external observer), but not from an 'emic' perspective (that of the participants)."* [BROMBERGER, HAYOT & AL. 1987: 41]

- Fourth, *"strict repetition within a sequential frame"* is missing in soccer; the action is always changing. Moreover, in the world of the game, idols *"are created from players who only several years before, were scarcely known, much less honoured"* whereas, in a conventional religion, the god or gods who are revered are fixed from the outset of the faith, and do not change.

- Finally, soccer lacks *"a representation of the world, of transcendence, of the beyond, [and] of salvation"* [BROMBERGER, HAYOT & AL. 1987: 41].

These three researchers conclude their fascinating discussion by elaborating the functions which a soccer match nevertheless fulfils. They conceded that although it embodies undeniable ritual dimensions, it lacks basic religiosity. Nevertheless, by *"legitimizing:* (a) *an extraordinarily broad range of determinative possibilities,* (b) *an occasion for the expression of social relations, even at their most contradictory, and* (c) *a privileged field affirming a specific set of values, the soccer match today offers a ritualized event* par excellence*, where a community mobilizes and dramatizes the essence of social and symbolic resources."* [BROMBERGER, HAYOT & AL. 1987: 41].[3]

c. In the beginning was Hockey, and Hockey was with Canada, and Hockey was Canada...

In the course of our own research, we have found only two studies that address the religious aspects of ice hockey.

The first is a small article by the Québec resident, Bernard Émond. An anthropologist by training, who subsequently achieved renown as a documentary film-maker, Émond has striven to unmask the ideological functioning of hockey. Sceptical about the predilections of other social scientists who have ascribed a religious value to the game, he has stated emphatically that to use religious discourse to speak about hockey is to tear the game from its actual social context (its status, in fact as a business enterprise) in order to concoct a symbolic product out of *"the* 'wonderful world of sports', [and so create] *"a naive, ahistorical setting for* [some] *humanistic utopia".* He insists that this conceptualization is neither innocent nor gratuitous, for it pretends that address *"objective social problems"* can be addressed by symbolic means. Thus *"a victory for* Le Canadien *in the playoffs* [is can be interpreted to] *to reaffirm the value of French-Canadian identity which the club embodies* [even though it is likely this had nothing to do with its immediate suc-

---

3. The authors allude to Lévi-Strauss, Cl. (1950). *Mythologiques: Le cru et le cuit.* Paris, Plon.

cess]. "Émond concludes by observing that the ideological impetus which undergirds the notion of hockey as a religion *"sanctions a depoliticized, ahistorical world, while transferring the roots of its signification out of its* [proper] *social domain".* [ÉMOND 1973: 81].

The second piece of research is an article by another Canadian, the historian, Tom Sinclair-Faulkner. Beginning with the rhetorical question (because it would seem that he has already made up his mind on this matter) – *"And what if being a hockey fan or player offers a way of being religious?"* – he adopts the concept of *"invisible religion"* proposed by the German sociologist, Thomas Luckmann,[4] to demonstrate that being a hockey fan or player in fact comprises a religious mode of being.

For Luckmann, reality is a symbolic universe that human beings create and by which they are created. It comprises four levels of meaning, that are organized hierarchically. At the lowest level, descriptions are drawn from what is immediately apparent. These are expressed, for example, in the statement, *"the grass is green".* At the second level, descriptions require some reflection: *"the grass needs water in order to grow".* At the third level, they become more complex and can be formulated as problems: '[how does] *a good farmer take care of his grass".* Finally, at the highest level, descriptions become *"massively problematical", "universally applied",* and [often] *"far removed from the concrete"* [SINCLAIR-FAULKNER 1977: 385]. This symbolic universe functions as a matrix, in the original sense of the term, allowing everyone to impart a meaning to their existence, to be born [to live] their humanity.

For Luckmann, to be human is to *"transcend oneself"* – that is to say, to transcend one's biological nature in order to become a conscious being, so as to approach the *"ultimate meaning"* of reality – that *"something more"* which Luckmann calls a *"sacred cosmos".* For him, religion is characterized by *"what humans do when they are human"* [SINCLAIR-FAULKNER 1977: 385-387]. When societies become complex, they tend to develop specific institutions whose function is to govern what it considers sacred – what Sinclair-Faulkner proposes to call its *"ecclesia".* His theoretical construct culminates with a decisive postulate: *"The crowning point of this sociological model of religion is Luckmann's observation that in a modern, highly complex society, a person possesses not one, but multiple symbolic universes, each offering him/her a sacred cosmos, supported by its own* 'ecclesia'. "[SINCLAIR-FAULKNER 1977: 388]

Convinced about the relevance of this conceptual framework, Sinclair-Faulkner proceeds to demonstrate that in Canada, ice hockey fulfils the role of an *"invisible religion".* He writes, *"There is a world of hockey, defined by its own symbolic universe and sustained by an* 'ecclesia'. *Those who live in this world organize their lives according to its meanings and requirements."* [SINCLAIR-FAULKNER 1977: 399]

4.Luckman, T. (1967). *The Invisible Religion: The Problem of Religion in Modern Society.* New York, Macmillan.

At its lowest level, ice hockey incorporates a number of material elements (for example, skates, a rink, and a puck) into its own symbolic universe. Furthermore, it comprises a specific set of attributes: it is fast-paced, intense, and *"full of colour, energy and danger"*; it involves two or three players in every defensive or offensive sequence, rather than the entire team; and it locates spectators very close to the action. Additionally, it shares a number of attributes with other sports: it honours the pleasures of the game, the aesthetics of physical activity, and the spirit of competition. However, it takes these to extreme limits, as illustrated in the following anecdote: When one of the Habs' legendary players, Maurice Richard, was asked about the team's unexpected defeat, by a journalist who reminded him of a saying by the father of the Olympic Games, Pierre de Coubertin, that *"the important thing is to participate"*, Richard replied sardonically, *"That Frenchman seems to me to have been born to lose."*[5] [SINCLAIR-FAULKNER 1977: 389].

Sinclair-Faulkner is unable to distinguish the next three levels proposed by Luckmann. But he is able to summarize the principal symbolic values of the game: *""In the hockey cosmos one is Canadian, one is manly (a quality which goes beyond sheer masculinity), and that one is excellent (by which I mean something that has more to do with winning than with the ancient Greek notion of arete"* [SINCLAIR-FAULKNER 1977: 391].

Obviously, these conditions depend in part on the game of hockey itself. The speed of the game requires *"trained reflexes"* more than it does *"reflective responses"*, and would seem to favour *"a level of aggressiveness far beyond the norm"* [SINCLAIR-FAULKNER 1977: 390]. But this *"symbolic universe"* is also forged by an *"ecclesia"*. The National Hockey League is obviously a major actor in the field; but it is not alone in defining the religion of hockey. For the body of doctrine that has come to define the cosmos of the game has emerged as well from books on the subject, from the speeches of coaches, from commentary provided by the media, and from the oral and written traditions of its players (both recounted in anecdotes, and in their life stories).

Sinclair-Faulkner describes five major features of this *"ecclesia"*. (1) It features Toronto as its capital, because the Hockey Hall of Fame is located there. (2) It depends upon clerics, whose hierarchical status is determined by the amount of time they commit to the sport, and the responsibilities they assume. (3) It manages its own disciplinary system, that is largely autonomous from the civil justice system. (4) It possesses a special language that is reserved for the initiated, and in which fans are permitted to swear or scream their frenzies [at players and officiants]. (5) And finally, it is able to integrate moments of crisis [into its world view] – making it capable of explaining, for example, the death of a player on the team, or the popular uprising that followed the infamous suspension of Maurice Richard in 1955.

---

5. Sinclair-Faulkner borrows this anecdote from O'Brien, A. (1967). *Fire Wagon Hockey*. Chicago, Follett: vi.

Sinclair-Faulkner poses one last question, that is perhaps crucial when considering whether hockey can be considered as a religion according to Luckmann's criteria: *"What happens when the individual leaves the world of hockey to try to construct his own 'invisible religion'? Does he avail himself of one or more of the meanings that are made* [specifically] *available in hockey?"* [SINCLAIR-FAULKNER 1977: 399]. The author responds affirmatively. He proposes *"eight values that hockey provides Canadians who are engaged in the construction of a Private Self"* [SINCLAIR-FAULKER 1977: 399]. These include: (1) A special time and space for social behaviour that would be considered inappropriate under other circumstances (including intimate contact between men); (2) a continuous biography, since one can play hockey throughout life; (3) life situations that offer clearly-defined responses to the problems that are posed; (4) an institution that is intermediate between the world of games and the world of work; (5) a model of masculinity; (6) a way of introducing colour and excitement into lives that may not be happy; (7) the possibility of escaping loneliness, while establishing [new] relationships, and (8) the pride of being a Canadian, because *"I, as a Canadian, am better than an American – even if I am not as rich, and am better than a European – even if I am not as cultivated"* [SINCLAIR-FAULKNER 1977: 400].

Chapter 3
A Habs' Religion? Which Religion?

As might be apparent from our review of these models, there is considerable variation in the authors' uses of the term *"religion"*. However, this should not be surprising, since *"more than a century of comparative study and reflection on* [the field of] *religion has* [thus far] *not resulted in a unique and satisfactory definition of its phenomenon... researchers seem to agree instead* [only] *on the extraordinary diversity to be found in the usages of the term, rather than on some universality"* [BASSET ET GISEL 1995: 1293]. Thus, any talk about *"the Hab's religion"* is necessarily incomplete. One must qualify this idea by specifying the kind of religion to which one is referring. The possibilities here are many and varied.

Without seeking to rank them, we will present six that seem particularly germane to the contexts of both the Habs and Quebec. At the same time, we will attempt not to succumb to the temptation, denounced by the Quebecer religious scholar, Guy Ménard, to distinguish *"between realities within a religious phenomenon that appear more 'visible' or more 'explicitly' religious than others,* [and] *which by virtue of appearing less, risk being deemed 'less religious' than them"* [MÉNARD 2006: 24].

a. Religion

The essence of religion, however one may choose to define it, would seem to consist in limning the reality of divinity, or of something transcendent, in the broadest sense. For *"religion, both in general and in particular, is a means of communication and of mediation, that is oriented in its principles and its practices, toward the perception of a reality that is radically other"* [BASSET ET GISEL 1995: 1295]. This definition, which would seem consensual, takes account of a long history of elaborate discussions about what constitutes a religion. The debate is scarcely new, for it has already endured for more than 2,000 years. Even the etymology of the term is problematic; for "religion" has been variously described as having arisen from two, ostensibly incompatible sources. A marked preference for one or the other, in an attempt to reconcile the two, only presupposes an ideological choice, that may not be immediately apparent.

In the 1st Century Before the Common Era, the Roman jurist, Cicero (*ca.* BCE 106-43), stated that the term, 'religio' derived from 'relegere' – meaning, "to reread, or to treat carefully". Thus he described "religion" as a concern for the scrupulous proofreading and understanding of texts, with a careful attention to their origins and founding rituals.[1] Three centuries later, Lactantius (*ca.* CE 240-320), a Christian rhetorician, attributed the term to another word, deriving it from 'religare' – "to tie together or connect". He proclaimed that the function of religion was to connect humans to God and to one another.[2] About a century later, St. Augustine (CE 354-430), believed to be the first person to have devoted an entire treatise to a theological analysis of this term and its cultural implications, strove to

---

1. In his book, *On the Nature of the Gods (De natura deorum)*, II. xxviii. 72, Cicero derives the term, 'religion' from 'relegere' (to treat or consider carefully; to review, reread or retrace): "*Those, on the other hand, who carefully reviewed, and so to speak, retraced, all the lore of ritual were called 'religious' from* 'relegere' *(to retrace or reread), like 'elegant' from* 'eligere' *(to select), 'diligent' from* 'diligere' *(to care for), 'intelligent' from* 'intellegere' *(to understand); for all these words contain the same sense of 'picking out' (*'legere'*) that is present in 'religious'* Cicero. *De natura deorum.* Translated and edited by H. Rackham (1923). Loeb Classical Library. Cambridge, Harvard University Press: v. 167

2. In his book, *Divine Principles (Divinae institutiones)*, IV. xxviii, Lactantius explains, "We are related and tied ('religati') to God by the bond of piety, and it is from this, and not as Cicero maintains, by careful consideration ('relegendo'), that 'religion' has received its name." LACTANCE. *Institutions divines.* Translated and edited by P. Pierre MONNAT. Sources Chrétiennes. Paris, Cerf: Books I, IV-VII, nos. 204-205, 326, 337, 377.

elicit a series of elements that were common to both meanings, while setting forth his own philosophical position.³

Notwithstanding Augustine's philological preferences, the etymological indeterminacy in the origins of the term bears relevance to our discussion about the Habs' religion. For if the team does in fact comprises a religion, then it we should be able to specify the radically other reality to which it points, and by which it permits its faithful not only to communicate, but to enter into some form of transcendent communion. Yet to begin, we need to determine the function it performs – whether it involves an act of careful attention, or one of connection?

A religion that carefully attends

From the perspective of "careful attention", the Habs' religion could be considered both positive and negative.

In its positive attribution, one might state that it has carefully attended to the issues of faithfulness and gratitude, memory and celebration, throughout its century-long history, and has cheerfully mingled myth with reality. This is well illustrated in the motto that is engraved on the team's locker room wall: *"To you from failing hands we throw the torch. Be yours to hold it high"*. From this perspective, the Hab's religion might be seen to comprise: (a) forms of communion – including [not only the] fellowship exemplified among its members (the fourteen players whose jersey were retired), but also among its supporters; (b) designated sacred places – including the Forum, where the team originated in 1924, and where it evolved into the formidable powerhouse it has since become; (c) specific celebrations – including 51 years of "Hockey Night" on Radio Canada, from 1952 to 2004)⁴; (d) highly commemorated events – such as the 24 Stanley Cups which the team has garnered; and (e) fetishistic objects – including the "Holy Flannel" (as the team's jersey has been called), emblazoned with the letters "C" and "H" (for "*le Club de Hockey*") ["Canadiens.com" 2008].

But in its faithfulness to tradition, however appropriate these attributes might seem (when recounting the team's accomplishments, so as to transmit its collective experience and memory to future generations) they can be-

---

3. In his work, *On True Religion (De vera religion)*, Augustine explores how man is capable of apperceiving the Divine through the careful focussing of his attention. Yet he also affirms that religion is an institution that binds man to God in time and history. Augustine. *De vera religion*. Translated and edited by J. Pegon (1951). Paris: Desclée De Brouwer / Études Augustiniennes: t. 8.

4. "It is worth noting that although only a few years have passed since hockey was introduced on television, enthusiasm for the sport has grown so much that the mere suggestion of diminishing its presence on the airwaves would result in a popular outcry. 'Hockey Night' has become a veritable institution, and the second religion of the Quebecer. An average of 1.5 million faithful participate in its worship services every Saturday evening." Black, F. (1997). *Habitants et glorieux: Les Canadiens de 1909 à 1960*. Laval, Mille Îles, 114.

come stultifying and moribund if they merely encourages superstitious attitudes and behaviours, or endlessly repeat vapid comments about past events that are only partially known. Under those conditions, the team's religion would seem to be almost a flight into the past, out of fear for the reality of the present. Limited to these behaviours, the Habs' religion would then share much in common with the "*obsessional neurosis*" by which Freud diagnosed religion. You will recall his memorable description: *"... one might venture to regard obsessional neurosis as the pathological counterpart of the formation of a religion, and to describe that neurosis as an individual religiosity, and religion as a universal obsessional neurosis"* [FREUD 1999: 44].

A religion that connects

From the perspective of "connection", the Habs' religion, could be viewed as forging a link (at the very least, a social link) to Montreal and Quebec. For it has served to connect or unite, in a single institution: Francophones and Anglophones, the city of Montréal and it suburbs, the young and the old, lifelong residents of Quebec and its recent immigrants, men and women, etc....

Should we rejoice in the fact that a Habs' religion seems to be capable of transcending differences? Of course we should. Yet we need to be cautious; for the unanimity it sustains may in fact be artificial, while the equality it create may likewise be illusory. It could be that the Habs' religion effectively hides our society's inconvenient truths, and makes us forget the many injustices and inequity which persist. In that respect, then it would seem more appropriate to label it as an "*opiate of the people*", to quote Karl Marx: You will recall Marx's sober observation, *"Religious suffering is first of all, an expression of real suffering, and secondly, a protest against real suffering. Religion is the sigh of the oppressed creature, the heart of a heartless world, and the spirit of a time without spirit. It is the opiate of the people."* [Marx 1843]. We could just as well imagine something better if it assumes a role no longer held by traditional religion (such as by the Catholic Church in Canada) whether that role is conferred by some vested authority after all, the principle of "*bread and circuses*" once served as a government program, or by some diffuse and impersonal will.

To offer yet another counter-argument, we might justifiably argue that instead of binding together, *The Habs*, like most other teams, inherently promotes division. For to be a supporter of one team (whether the Toronto *Leafs*, the Vancouver *Canucks*, the Edmonton *Oilers*, the Calgary *Flames*, or the Ottawa *Senators)* often implies and for some, necessarily so that one ignores, despises and even hates every other opposing team, as well as the cities they represent, their players and their supporters, in a more or less subtle hierarchy. Even death (or at least that of a franchise) may not be enough to end this sense of rivalry. Thus the supporters of the *Nordiques* of Quebec City (another team from the same province as The Habs, who never fared as well), came to hate the Habs on principle, after their club was sold and transferred to Colorado, and continue to await the resurrection of their beloved club with its distinctive *fleur-de-lis* jersey.[5]

However, it may be possible to achieve reconciliation at a different level – provided, at least, there is an available scapegoat. This has happened in the past, for example, when the Habs have played on behalf of Québec against the rest of Canada, or when all Canadian franchise teams play against the US, or when the Canadian National Team plays against other countries (and against Russia in particular). As Émond noted, at a symbolic level "*the problem of Québec's independence*[6] *was 'settled' during the tournament of Russia vs. Canada* [in 1972]*: Francophone and Anglophone athletes* [and their supporters] *united, upon being confronted by a graver threat: that of the spectre of Communism.*" [ÉMOND 1973: 83].

Notwithstanding its possible divisiveness, we believe that the rivalry, and even the hatred, which the team may reinforce, do not outweigh the Habs' distinctive religiosity. Quite the opposite! For whether one is willing to admit it or not, divisiveness, rivalry and hatred are also facts religion, and underlie the fanaticism of its zealots. In that respect, we might even consider the Habs to be pre-eminently religious, because it ascribes an absolute worth to dying (in the figurative sense at least) for the team.

b. Institutional Religion

The essence of a religion invariably transcends its particular manifestations – whether embodied in Judaism, Christianity, Islam, Hinduism, or something else. That essence is shared by the traditions within a given faith (so that within Christianity, for example, one can find Catholic, Orthodox

---

5. This dispute arose in part from, or culminated in, a match in 1984, when *the Habs* played *Les Nordiques*, on Friday, April 20th – which happened to be Good Friday. The match, which was later described as "the darkest [match] in the history of the game", ended in a 20 minute brawl. "Everywhere across the ice rink, players chased one another. Duels broke out with unprecedented violence." See Chabot, J.-F. (2003) "Le match le plus sombre de l'histoire." Webpage, consulted on 2 June 2008 at: http://www.radio-canada.ca/Sportsv1/matchsdesanciens/nouvelles/200304/09/001-VendrediSaint.asp. To see videos of the match, consult, "La Bataille Générale Canadiens – Nordiques du Vendredi Saint" (1984). Webpage, consulted on 2 June 2008 at: http://www.youtube.com/watch?v=hqsVXIhwAzA

6. "During a previous era, the dream of an independent, sovereign Quebec invoked strong emotion, and had an almost religious fervour to it. This was especially the case in regions where the major proportion of the population were blue-collar Francophones employed by predominantly Anglophone industrialists. Following the post WW2 years, Quebec's blue-collar workforce saw himself or herself as being oppressed economically, politically and culturally by the province's Anglophone population. Freedom for the pro-sovereignist Francophone population meant freedom from Anglophone economic and political oppression and freedom from Anglophone cultural domination and assimilation." Valentine, H. (2002), "The Emperor's Derrière: The Changed Vision of Quebec Independence," *Le Québec Libre*, No. 104 (Montreal, May 11, 2002), 1.

and Protestant traditions), and likewise subsists within the institutions of those respective confessions (so that there is a distinctive Roman Catholic Church, a Maronite Church, a Patriarchate of Moscow and All Russia, various Presbyterian Churches, or likewise, the United Church of Canada. The religious nature of each of these is defined, more or less adequately by the specific forms, dogmas, beliefs, ethics, practices and rites that each faith, tradition and confession comes to embody. "*Worship is probably the most basic element of religion; but moral conduct, right belief, and participation in religious ceremonies are usually also constituent elements of the religious life – both as practiced by believers and worshippers, and as commanded by sages and scriptures.*" [ENCYCLOPÆDIA BRITANNICA, n.d.]

In considering the Habs as a religion, it would be well to note the features it holds in common with other institutionalized religions. In this regard, it might be possible to view it as a church alongside other similarly construed churches (such as the Québec *Remparts*, the Boston *Bruins*, or *CSKA* Moscow. Likewise, it might be possible to consider it as belonging to a confession) that of the National Hockey League – which coexists with other confessions (including the Quebec Major Junior Hockey League, and the Continental Hockey League[7]), that sometimes compete, and sometimes exist in comity, with one another. Similarly, in relation to the team, the International Ice Hockey Federation could be viewed in a role that is correlative to that of the World Council of Churches. Moreover, the Habs might be seen as differing from other traditions of sports – such as those of field hockey, football, soccer, or baseball.

In defining it still more precisely, we could consider the degree to which its values coincide with or diverge from those prized in other sports (similar to the currents found in other religions), including whether it is liberal, traditional, mystical or fundamentalist; whether it is an Olympic or non-Olympic sport, an elite or a popular sport, a professional or an amateur sport, etc.

To those who might object that the classifying the Habs as a religion seems far-fetched, and that the commitment of sports fans is not commensurate with that of the faithful, we could point out that there are varying degrees of involvement in hockey, just as there are varying degrees of involvement in the Church. Following Daniele Hervieu-Léger, we might here distinguish here three possible levels of involvement: that of (1) "*the group of consumers*" – those who seek "*an institution that is both capable of, and legitimate in, issuing symbolic goods*"; (2) that of "*the group of practitioners*" – those who seek "*a form of spiritual training which refers them on a continuing rather than occasional basis to a set of practices, rules of life, and ethics that have a religious basis;* and (3)

---

7. The Continental Hockey League was established in 1972, and remained in existence until 1987. The All American Hockey League succeeded it in 1988, which survived only a year before it, too, was succeeded by the East Coast Hockey League, which has continued in its place since 1989.

that of *"the group of utopian activists"* – those believers who seek *"to transform themselves with the hope of attaining a new state of life that will engage their entire existence"* [FLIPO 2003: 131].[8]

Mutatis mutandi, we might wish to map comparable levels of involvement onto the faithful of the Habs. The *"consumers"* would include those whose celebrations with the team are limited principally to the games, though occasionally also, to the team's victory processions on St-Catherine Street in Montreal. The *"practitioners"* would include those who arrange their lives according to the fortunes and misfortunes of the team; while the *"activists"* would include those who consecrate their entire existence to the *"Holy Flannel"*.

Following this schema, we should expect to find the greatest number of faithful at that level which requires the least amount of their commitment – the consumers. Yet how are we to conceive of the players, the coaches and the managers? We would expect to find them at the second level – that of the practitioners –, although one might hope their commitments would rise to the third – the activists. Yet even here, their degrees of involvement would likely vary. While some of them might be deeply observant and unquestionably committed to the Habs, others are likely to be less so. For still others, playing for the Habs might represent only one opportunity among others in their lives, or even just a short-term engagement for which they have no long-term expectations.

c. Popular Religion

As stated previously, the essence of religion is not confined to the institutions which come to embody its reality. Rather, it flows within and actuates them – at times overflowing, at times contracting, while forever nuancing, their reality. This phenomenon is particularly prominent in what has come to be known as *"popular religion"*. "*The notion of popular religion gains its significance in societies where religious authorities strive to ensure the strict observance of orthodoxy and orthopraxis; standing in opposition to the official religion, the popular religion consists in the actual or lived religiosity* [of the people] *at the level of* [their] *representations, sentiments and customs.*" [MAÎTRE 2007] It is popular both because it emanates from the masses, who give birth to it, and because it suits them, since they, in turn, consume it.

That the Habs suit the people would seem indisputable. Suffice it to say that it plays to sold-out crowds, and has continuously held 21,273 spectators captive since the beginning of the 2004 season. But do the Habs emanate from the people? In response to this question, we can envisage two diametrically opposed answers.

---

[8]. These categories were introduced in Hervieu-Léger, D. (2001). *La religion en miettes, ou la question des sectes.* Paris, Calmann-Lévy.

the Habs could be considered a popular religion, because it falls under a distinct authority incarnated in the National Hockey League. The fact that the Francophone (or at least bilingual) culture of the team has managed to survive the Anglophone culture of the League all these years, lends credence to this proposition. By the ways in which its members communicate and live with one another, under a set of forms they have chosen, the managers, the players, the fans, and the media, have together engendered a distinct social entity. What most distinguishes the Habs, and enhances its qualification as a popular religion, is its Quebecer character. It is unique as much for the language it uses (Quebecer French), as for the players and the trainers it selects (Quebec residents), and for its distinctive style of play – commonly referred to as that of the "*Flying Frenchmen*".

But is this sufficient? Certainly the Habs possess a unique set of popular attributes. It promotes a family-centred form of hockey, which stands in contrast, for example, to that of the Philadelphia *Flyers*, who exemplify a more virile form of the game that is marketed as a form combat.[9] However, the differences between these two teams are less blatant in other respects. The Habs no longer have the privilege of hiring the best players from Quebec, as it did forty years ago. Rather, today it counts on its roster: Canadians, Americans, Russians and Fins – all of whom would probably be more comfortable speaking English to one another than in the team's chosen *lingua franca* of French.

While the Habs may seem like a popular religion in some respects, it cannot be readily distinguished from its parent institution in other respects. In fact, from an institutional perspectives, the organization could not even exist outside of the National Hockey League, which dictates its liturgy and its dogmas. And that is precisely what bothers some of its supporters, who would like it to become more popular (that is to say, more Quebecer), and less institutional – that is, less representative of the NHL's American sports culture.

At this point, it seems worth exploring another possibility – one in which the team itself exercises the role of a religious authority. In this case, we might consider the team to be the guardian of the temple which fixes the doctrine and liturgy not simply of its members, but of hockey in Montreal, or in Québec more generally. Popular religion often arises as a revolt against the established religious institutions in a society. It is thus not uncommon to find among its number, dissidents (or "heretics" in the eyes of the established religion), who dare to celebrate the faith outside the rites that were officially established. In this scenario, if the hockey of the Habs were considered the official religion, then the teams which engage in differing forms of hockey at the local, national and international levels would themselves be deemed as popular religions. For example, it is not difficult to conceive

---

9. Interview with Vincent Lucier, Sales Manager for Le Canadien de Montreal (26 November 2007). In 2008, the Philadelphia *Flyers* entered the playoffs against *the Habs*, swearing revenge. See Philadelphia Flyers. (2008). "Reserve Your Playoff Tickets!" Webpage consulted on 15 April 2008 at: http://flyers.nhl.com.

of these other teams acting against the dogmas espoused by the Habs, and playing the game simply for the joy of playing, or as revering idols other than those who wear the coveted "CH" jersey. Note that the practice of popular religion does not preclude these possibilities; so that the rites and beliefs of a minority faith tradition can gain pre-eminence among the other traditions in a society, and in that respect, serve as the official doctrinal standard, while in other respects, remaining but a dissident voice that other traditions would prefer not to heed.

d. Implicit Religion

Let us consider another type of religious formation – that of "*implicit religion*". The inventor of this concept, the British scholar, Edward I. Bailey, defined it according to three attributes, for each of which he highlighted a series of problems that were posed.

- Very broadly, an "*implicit religion*", like any other religion, first of all, entails a commitment that encompasses "*a whole range of experiences which are more or less deeply conscious, reflective and deliberate*" [BAILEY 1966: 16], with the following caveat: "*the term involves a conscious and voluntary commitment, or makes reference to something largely unconscious, – to a kind of inevitable legacy – dare we say, one that is imposed on us without our knowledge? Well, actually, it is both.*" [BAILEY 1966: 16].

- Next, an implicit religion functions as an "*integrating focus/foci*" [BAILEY 1996: 17]. This second definition is "*the problem of singular and plural. Is the study of implicit religion concerned with individual events, or rather with collective phenomena? Here again, we must reply: with one and the other.*" [BAILEY 1996: 17]. The structural framework which unites the multiple dimensions of an individual's being and his existence, is at the same time chosen by him, and/or is recommended by his community.

- Finally, an implicit religion correlates "*intensive concerns with extensive effects*" [BAILEY 1996: 18]. It must affect the totality of the believer's existence. "*So that it remains relevant in this respect, the phenomenon must have a particularly deep and significant impact on the individual, or on the group it affects*" [BAILEY 1996: 18].

We might be able to categorize the Habs as an implicit religion if we can demonstrate its integration of these three aspects. Undoubtedly, it entails a commitment for many people – a commitment that can be witnessed in public by the wearing of a helmet, or a jersey marked with the letters "CH"; or by a fan's declaration of the player to whom s/he is loyal; or by hanging a Habs' flag from the window of her car or the balcony of his apartment. Yet more importantly, the team offers a means for the socialization of its supporters, and can impact their lives outside of the rink.

But moving beyond this more or less abstract description, do the Habs function as an implicit religion? We are not persuaded that it does, because those who live solely for the team, or who organize their lives around its existence down to the most minute details (vis-à-vis their loves, their family, their career, their finances, their spirituality, etc) are extraordinarily few in number, if they exist at all...

However, Bailey adds a comment that may be crucial for our consideration of this possibility: "*If... the terms of our third definition (concerns, effects, etc.) are multiple, that is because they signify the plurality of figures who share in this implicit religion – as much on the level of consciousness, as in the social breadth of the phenomenon, and kind of sociability, it generates... To belong to a single 'universe of reference' would seem to conjure a bygone era in our societies, when their size was more modest and their organization was relatively simple*" [BAILEY 1996: 18-19]. These considerations suggest that the Habs' religion should not be exclusivist, but should allow its faithful to maintain multiple commitments, to entertain several intensive engagements, and even to increase their integrative foci. This possibility seems more consistent with reality.

e. Civil Religion

There is another concept that might prove useful in understanding the status of the Habs – that of "civil religion". Formulated by Jean-Jacques Rousseau in Switzerland in the 18th Century, it expresses "*the dimensions of religious faith and the politics of social relationships*" [CAMPICHE 1995: 1318]. [While perhaps European in its origins,] it is in America that the highest form of civil religion has been found. "*Very generally, civil religion [there] describes how Americans, throughout the history of their nation, created a collective national identity, while imparting a sacred value to set of secular symbols, rites and institutions*"[EVANS 2002a: 14].

But the concept has deeper implications. Robert Bellah has shown that it expresses two fundamental convictions in the United States: (1) confidence in a God who blesses America, and (2) a certainty that Americans serve, both individually and collectively, as instruments of Divine Providence – that is, that they are responsible for how the will of God is fulfilled on earth [BELLAH 1967]. For historical reasons, American civil religion developed out of Judeo-Christianity; however it allows the coexistence of other religions. The sole requirement is that these other religions espouse the existence of a divine being, no matter which. We thus might rephrase the American motto [that is engraved on its dollar bills] to read: "*In any God we trust*[10]! The logical conclusion (or demonic perversion) of this civil religion is the possible transposition from "*a promise for America (from a transcendent divinity), to the promise of America (as a self-transcending nation)*" [EVANS 2002a: 27].

We might be able to make the Habs the civil religion of Quebec, if we could demonstrate its power to unite or federate. There seems little doubt about that power, for reasons we have already enumerated. But to comprise a civil religion, it should also meet two other conditions proposed by Bellah. Does it succeed there as well?

First of all, do the Habs witness to God's blessing on Quebec? We feel inclined to say "yes," and to defend the idea that that the team nurtures this conviction. In a province that has long been mispriced (the traditional Quebecer proverb, "*né pour un petit pain*",[11] has long been deemed to attest to the limited ambitions of its residents), the unparalleled success of the team has become a rare mark of pride for its people, and a sign that God has not forsaken "*la Belle Province*".

But the second condition seems more problematic. Are there really individuals who believe that the Habs are Quebec's gift to the world? Even if we were to concede that anything is possible, this seems an extravagant claim. However, if we broaden our horizons to the survey the field of hockey more generally, it is possible to affirm the team lays claim to one or more of the three attributes traditionally defined as being "Canadien" – at least, in the original sense of this word. Two of those attributes (the French language and the Catholic religion) even if they are now common in Quebec, and have come to characterize the team, were not native to the country, but were imported from France in the 16th Century. However, the third attribute (hockey) belongs to Quebec, and to Quebec alone; for the game originated here. Indeed, the first match in the history of game took place on 3 March 1875 not simply in Quebec, but in Montreal – at the Victoria Skating Rink. Accordingly, the Habs could meet Bellah's second criteria; for in

---

10. "Speaking at the Council of Foreign Relations in Manhattan, the imam, Feisal Abdul Rauf [the chairman of the Cordoba Initiative, which seeks to build an interfaith community center and mosque at Ground Zero in lower Manhattan] ... recalled his shock, as a teenager, upon arriving with his Egyptian family in the 1960s, at a Time magazine cover asking, "Is God Dead?"– and his later realization that the United States was a religious country where religion was optional. "In that sense, you could say I found my faith in this country," he said. "For me, Islam and America are organically bound together. This is not my story alone. The American way of life has helped many Muslims make a conscious decision to embrace their faith. That choice is precious. And that is why America is precious." BARNARD, A. (2010). "Imam Says He's Open to Options on Islamic Center," *The New York Times*, 14 September 2010, A22.

11. The phrase, can be translated literally as "*born worthy of receiving only a small bread roll*", or figuratively as "*having little ambition*" and consequently, "*destined to insignificance*". It originated in a now archaic translation of a passage in the Bible: JOSHUA 9: 23.

a sense it is Quebec's gift to the world – witness the countless number of coaches and players from "*la Belle Province*" who now figure on hockey teams around the globe!

f. Quasi-Religon

Finally, we wish to present a concept introduced by the German theologian, Paul Tillich, in the 1930's – that of "*quasi-religion*". Tillich used this term to describe the dominant political ideologies of his time – liberal humanism, fascism, and communism. For him, all of these were "*secular religions*". They "*did not refer to a transcendent principle or being, but rather proposed answers to questions about the meaning of existence... They had all the characteristics of religions. However, they did not admit to being religious, even though they served this function in quite profound ways*" [GOUNELLE & REYMOND 2005: 90-91].

The distinction between "*religion*" and "*quasi-religion*" that Tillich proposed is two-fold. First of all, there must be a concern for the presence (or the absence) of an explicit reference to transcendence. Being secular, quasi-religions do not profess the existence of anything transcendent but instead proclaim its absence. Secondly, there is concern for form that is, with the proper manner for personal and public expression of this conviction. It is here, however, that the distinction between religion and quasi-religion begins to crumble, and can even disappear. For although quasi-religions disavow its reality, they do function as religions in several specific ways. Both are based on a set of dogmas and beliefs; both refer to a set of founding texts; both depute officiants to guard and preserve what is deemed holy; both are punctuated by rituals celebrated in symbolic spaces, etc. In fact, both conjoin "*within the confines of space and time, the contradictory claim of immanence and the call for transcendence*" [MÜLLER 2004]. Traditionally, it is this latter feature which has most commonly characterized "religion", while the former tends to be associated with "quasi-religion"; yet both these attributes can be found in each.

To make the Habs a quasi-religion would seem promising, because it is then freed from the constraint of having to reference a form of transcendence. Even so, it still must provide a particular response to questions about the meaning of existence. Unlike the great ideologies cited by Tillich, the Habs do not pretend to claim that role. It assumes no responsibility in reducing injustice or establishing equality within society. It presents itself merely as a hockey team, or viewed from another light, as a business engaged in marketing sports entertainment. But in so doing, it also promotes a set of values that some people use in building their lives. For example, with regard to the players it espouses the values of: (1) teamwork (every player assumes a role that is appropriate to his particular talents, and that helps to advance the team's reputation); (2) the need to surpass oneself, and the discipline, and ruthless selection, which this involves (only the best players are able to qualify for the Habs, and those who join the team are typically able to meet its demands); (3) the receipt of rewards according to merit (every players knows that his worth depends on the athletic and economic value of his performance); (4) submission to the laws of the marketplace (even a great player incurs the risk of being traded or dismissed on short notice); and (5) the legitimation of violence (within the rules allowed of course, or just beyond these). Perhaps we should also add (6) a taste for victory; though during the last few seasons, the team has had to show how to deal graciously with defeat – a virtue that is no less useful in society than it is in sports.

Chapter 4
What is the Relationship between Sports and Religion?

If we accept sports as a form of religion (in whatever sense we ascribe to this term) it becomes legitimate to ask how it might relate to other religions (whatever their institutional configurations) – whether popular, implicit, or civil; or likewise, to quasi-religions.

In this spirit, we propose to consider four models, that are delineated according to the closeness of relationships they maintain between sports and religion. We will assess the appropriateness of each model in comparing the Habs (as that sports entity which interests us most) to the Catholic Church (as the major religious institution of Quebec). We would remark in advance that the first two models do not make a distinction between the sport of religion, and the religion of sport (or sports), while the latter two seek to decisively separate sports from religion. Whichever model we choose, the question of the articulation between this sports/religion coupling with other dimensions of society (such as culture, politics and economics) – will remain open.

a. Inclusivism

In our first model, both sports and religion can be viewed as variously included within one another – hence our adoption of the term, *"inclusive"*. This type of relationship has two varieties – one in which sports is conceived as an aspect of religion, and the other in which religion is conceived as an aspect of sports.

To conceive of sports as an aspect of religion implies not only that it exists within the context of the latter, but also that it is coherent and congruent with the principles of religion. For the believer, sports can offer an occasion for: (a) the public affirmation of his/her faith (which is prone to gaining increased significance through the mediatisation that surrounds the broadcasting of sports); (b) by explicit gestures (such as by making the Sign of the Cross upon entrance to the ice rink, or kneeling in prayer on the track); (c) by one's manner of dress – including wearing a bandana to cover one's hair (whether on the field or on a tatami mat), or lifting one's jersey in order to reveal a message printed on one's undershirt (the popular phrase, "Jesus loves you"); or (d) by the refusal to profane religious holidays by not playing on them (whether the Sabbath of Judaism or Christianity, or conceivably even, Ramadan in Islam).

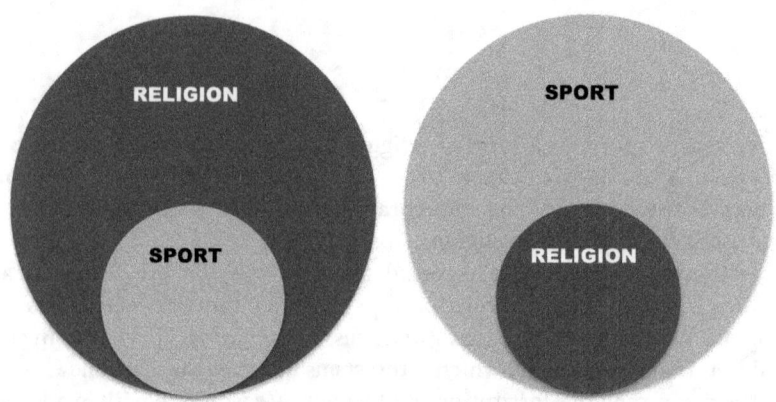

Figure 1: Inclusivism

In religious institutions, sports can become a tool used to transmit specific doctrines; it gains utility in teaching and learning the faith, as well as in the promulgation of the ethical behaviour which the religion seeks to advance. One thinks here of the use of sports in the educational tradition of the Jesuits, and their desire to train a person's body, heart, mind and spirit (*"mens sana in corpore sano"*)[1] – first, through gymnastics, and then, through

---

1. The phrase translates as: "a sound mind in a healthy body".

sports. Likewise; one thinks of American Protestantism, and the campaigns for *"muscular Christianity"*,[2] which began in the gymnasiums of the YMCA during the Victorian Era; or again of basketball – which developed under the ministerial impetus of the Canadian, James Naismith, who held a diploma in theology from the Presbyterian College of McGill University in Montreal; or finally of Pope John Paul II, (at least before the pitiful end of his life), who *"had a pool installed in the papal residence, and who regularly engaged in skiing, to unwind from the pressures of his work, and whose many teachings about sports attempted to provide the Church with leadership in this area"* [KERRIGAN 1992: 253].

But conversely, it is possible to conceive of religion as simply an aspect of sports, and to exploit its resources for athletic ideals. An example here would be the spectacular soccer goal made by Argentinean player, Diego Maradona, in the quarter finals of the World Cup Soccer Tournament in Mexico in 1996 in which he accidentally used his hand, though claimed that his team's victory over England was due to "the hand of God" (*la mano de Dios*).[3] Some athletes resort to religion – using the Sign of the Cross, for example, in order to optimize their performance, as if it were a form of training, diet or even doping. This then poses the question: can praying before playing be considered a form of cheating? Whatever one's view on this matter, by emphasizing the religious aspects of athleticism, the sports industry is able to increase the marketability of their product (there are few atheists or agnostics who do not believe in the gods of the stadium), as well as their consumer loyalty, while making the stadium into a veritable church, temple, mosque or synagogue.

Inclusivism would seem appropriate in the context of Quebec, because the Catholic Church uses (or did use, up until the Quiet Revolution[4]) the Habs to its advantage. Whenever players or coaches of the team have publicly affirmed their membership in the Catholic Church, the Church has benefitted. Some examples of this include the public attestations offered by the team's players: Jean Béliveau, who came from a very Catholic family; or Jacques Demers, known for his regular pilgrimages to the Shrine of St.

---

2. See HALL, D. E., (ed.) (1994). *Muscular Christianity: Embodying the Victorian Age*. Cambridge, Cambridge University Press; and Putney, C. (2001). *Muscular Christianity: Manhood and Sports in Protestant America, 1880-1920*. Cambridge, Harvard University Press.

3. See the YouTube video for "Maradona - Hand of God Goal" at: http://www.youtube.com/watch?v=uozjx4MAHzk.

4. "The Quiet Revolution is the name given to a period of Quebec history extending from 1960 to 1966, and corresponding to the tenure of office of the Liberal Party of Jean Lesage. The term appears to have been coined by a Toronto journalist who, upon witnessing the many and far reaching changes taking place in Quebec, declared that what was happening was nothing short of a revolution, albeit a quiet one." BELANGER, C. (2006). "Events, Issues and Concepts of Quebec History: The Quiet Revolution". Webpage consulted on 10 August 2010: http://faculty.marianopolis.edu/c.belanger/quebechistory/events/quiet.htm.

Anne de Beaupré; or likewise, Tomas Plekanec, and his insistence on crossing himself each time he entered the ice rink – all of which directly or indirectly legitimized the value of the Catholic Church in Canadian society, while contradicting of the stereotype of Christianity as a religion of the lost.[5] Inclusivism can even convert its symbolic capital into real money, and make a mere object used by a member of the team (such as a jersey or a hockey stick) into a marketing product from which the team directly profits.

But in return, the Habs exploit (or has exploited), the Catholic Church, as the dominant moral authority of Quebec, because it is difficult for it to assume that authority itself in a world that has become increasingly secular and more religiously diverse. As one example here, beyond any personal pleasure that he or the Church may gain by watching the team play, the Habs unquestionably benefit from the visibility of Cardinal Jean-Claude Turcotte at so many of its matches and other celebrations.

b. Syncretism

Syncretism lies at the heart of the second model we propose to consider. For Christianity, the idea of being defined as *"an amalgam of Christian and traditional religious practices"* [CHANSON 2001] undoubtedly holds a pejorative connotation. This derives from a *"theological controversy maintained by those who oppose an authentic and original Christianity, to a 'syncretic' faith that has incorporated various pagan influences which have persisted up to the present day"* [SABATUCCI 2007]. But following the classical definition of *"syncretism"* as the *"fusion of two or more religions, or two or more cults, into a single religious or cultural phenomenon"* [SABATUCCI 2007] the term more neutrally refers to the mixing of two entities, which results in the creation of a new entity that is no longer one or the other, but rather something new, yet which nevertheless bears characteristics from each.

In syncretism, attributes of both sports and religion could be fused into an amalgam that emerges as a real, authentic and original religion of sports. The Olympic Games represents what appears to be one of the most successful examples of this phenomenon. The founder of the Olympic movement, Pierre de Coubertin, never denied that the Olympics were for him, first and foremost, a religion – that is to say, an *"accession to a higher ideal of life, a striving for perfection"* ["Pierre de Coubertin" 2008]. Together with his successors in the International Olympic Committee, he created a new religion founded on elements (specifically, beliefs, symbols, words, rituals, etc.) that were borrowed from Greco-Roman, Judeo-Christian, and Germano-Scandinavian religions. These were in turn reorganized, reinterpreted, and readapted to serve the specific aims and context of the Games. At this stage, it is con-

---

5. On this count, see the discussion of Montherlant below, and MEUNIER, R. (1988). "La conception religieuse du sport chez H. de Montherlant" in Sports, *arts et religions*. G. ANDREU (ed.). Paris, Éditions C. R. Staps: 40-46.

ceivable that the Olympics may eventually come to incorporate aspects of even Eastern religious traditions before it finishes evolving. Yet what is important to note is that it has created a new sport, that is mostly unlike any that existed before.

Figure 2: Syncretism

The usefulness of this model in describing the relationship between the Habs and the Catholic Church, seems questionable, however. Neither Quebecois Catholicism, nor the form of hockey practiced by the Habs, are so unique as to allow one to affirm that they have resulted in a new form of "sporting religion".

c. Dimorphism

A third way to link sports and religion would be to consider what the Canadian historian, Cornelius Jaenen, has referred to as "*dimorphism*".[6] Describing the responses offered by Native Americans to the Christian missionaries who sought to convert them to their faith, he explained "*that a member of a First Nation could adhere to the new religion and a system of traditional beliefs at the same time*" [JAENEN 1985: 185]. Jaenen proposed a typology, ranking the eight kinds of responses that were offered, which ranged from "*belligerent rejection*" to "*full acceptance*". He stated that the majority of those Natives who were reputedly "*converted*" actually maintained "*religious dimorphism*" –

---

[6] In a paper delivered at the University of Toronto in 1984, Jaenen, who was then a professor at the University of Ottawa, suggested a model to explain how a First Nation individual could align himself to a new religion, while maintaining his traditional belief system. He called this compartmentalized dualism, "*religious dimorphism*" Jaenen C. (1985). "Amerindian Responses to French Missionary Intrusion, 1611-1760: A Categorization". Thèmes Canadiens / Canadian Issues 7: 182-197: 185.

"which is the simultaneous acceptance of their old ways and the new religion, with each being separated and used as need and circumstance dictated" [JAMES 1999: 4-5].

If syncretism can serve to blend sports and religion, dimorphism, by contrast, *"ensures 'compartmentalization', particularly when the beliefs involved are mutually contradictory"* [JAMES 1999: 4-5] Dimorphism permits the selection of doctrinal beliefs from each constituent religion, allowing the believer to confront life and cope with particular situations [with utmost expedience].

In the dimorphic model, sports and religion are not confounded, but rather remain distinct and separate, yet related to one another. However, for dimorphism to exist, there must be a area of commonality between the two bodies of religious phenomena; this is its *sine qua non*. The size of that area may vary, and the commonalities may be few; but they must exist. It is in relation to these shared points that the two underlying religions are able to express diverse and even contradictory beliefs.

Against a backdrop of common hope or belief in providence or fate, dimorphism between sports and religion permits the simultaneous valuing of love, respect and solidarity, amidst the exercise of violence and hatred. We will not attempt to prejudge in which culture the faithful will choose to enact their love or their violence. There are those who rage in stadiums, or who love in church; while there are others who express their violence in religion and their solidarity in sports...

At the same time, we have no intention of hiding our preference in our review of these religious models. In our view, the dimorphic model appears the most appropriate in expressing the relationships between the Catholic Church and the Habs. It simultaneously takes note of the differences between these two religions, while recognizing the values they share in common.

Culturally, the Francophone nature of both the hockey team and the Catholic Church in Quebec would seem to be the nexus between these two institutions. Even though the Habs have been a bicultural organization since its founding, and that Protestantism arrived in Quebec with the earliest French explorers and colonizers, both have succeeded in imposing the language of French on Quebec as part of its identity. For that reason, both have emerged as living incarnations of the Province. Notwithstanding the undeniable success of each, and in spite of the team's epithet as, "The Glorious", which some might see as more appropriate to the Church, the theological nexus between the two lies with Good Friday. That is because both the team and the Church prize forms of dolorism or religious anguish – witness the team's motto in which "bruised arms ... carry aloft the flame" of its perseverance, or the Catholic Church's crucifix in which a tortured Christ offers salvation.

But moving from these points of convergence, both religions offer beliefs that at some points are divergent and contradictory, while at other points, complementary. An ardent supporter of the Habs, who is also a member of the Catholic Church, can compartmentalize his/her beliefs, while benefitting from the respective strength of each religion, according to his/her needs and circumstances. Thus a believer might make reference to the religion of the team in his professional life, as a way of justifying his compulsion to fight, or to impose his will on others at their expense, while simultaneously reaffirming his faith in the Catholic Church in order to justify his need to forgive and be forgiven. He could likewise reaffirm his adherence to both religions whenever he sacrifices himself for the team, the Church, or even the community, while avoiding schizophrenia.

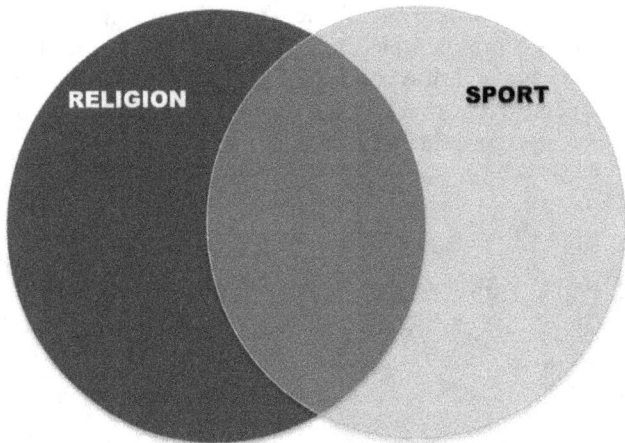

Figure 3: Dimorphism

d. Exclusivism

Finally, religion and sports may share no points in common. Such a position, which is radically exclusivist, obliges the faithful to choose one path or the other.

In his novels, the French writer, Henri de Montherlant, deliberately excludes positive religion (or more specifically, Christianity) from his conception of sports. In his view, Christian morality is a morality of the weak, the poor, and the vengeful: "*Like the Christ it has chosen, if humanity has been crucified, that is because it wants this. For you can always cry out to him, with the good sense of the Pharisees, 'You have only to descend from the cross'*" (Mt. 27: 41-43; Mk. 15: 31-32) [MONTHERLANT 1954: 147]. Montherlant opposes a morality of sports with a morality of the victors, whom, he claims, alone have the option of being generous. "*With strength, there is a place for everything: setbacks, forgetfulness, kindness, charity, nerve, poisons, dizziness... And all these, which are dangerous without strength, become virtuous with it. With strength, there is laughter; with strength, there is the game; with strength, there is freedom. Anyone who knows his strength, knows paradise*" [Montherlant 1954: 148]. Montherlant tends to make sports into a true religion. "*The runners of the 500 [meter race] get into place. Peyrony skips, with the solemn face, the lowered eyebrows, of a boy who approaches the communion table. Yes that is the dignity of the young official; it seems only natural because his religion is here. And his body, taut from top to bottom, appears prepared in every respect, befitting one who approaches the altar."* [Montherlant 1954: 138].[7]

The radical differentiation of religion from sports, and their independence from one another, can have two contrasting effects. It can eliminate the divine that is found within human capacity; or it can reintroduce the divine, which then assumes a dimension of human transcendence. *"The whole question will be to know how, over the course of time, this power was conceived and shared between the human* and the divine – whether as a superhuman power that was given by the gods, which thus is divine; or as a mortal power that was created by man, and thus is human." [GARASSINO 1992: 67]. It is in line with this perspective, that sports sometimes becomes a rival to religion, and can be perceived as a threat to its god.

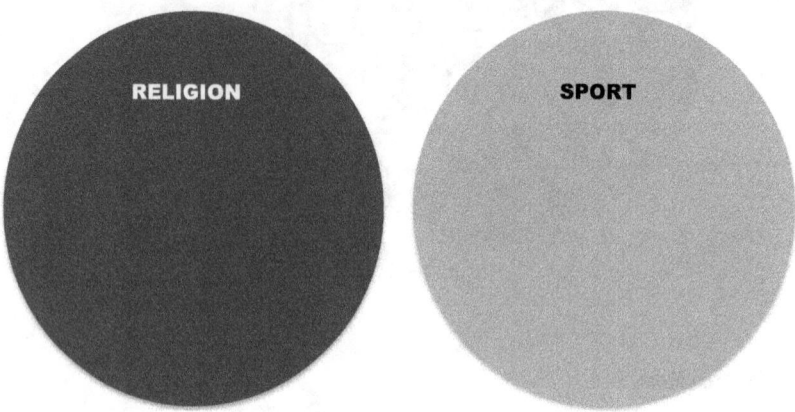

Figure 4: Exclusivism

Religion has tried (or rather, certain religions, or certain tendencies within religion, have tried) to exclude sports, because it deems it idolatrous. While Hellenism may have promoted sports, Judaism expressed reservations about it. The Greeks advocated an ideal of beauty; for them, nudity was required by the athlete, and glorified in the Olympics. But the Jews favoured an ideal of purity, in which nakedness and circumcision instead conveyed a sense of shame (as recorded in the Book of Genesis). However, it is worth noting that in the 12th Century, in his *Treatise on the Medical Aphorisms of Moses*, and his *Treatise on the Preservation of Health*, Rabbi Moshe ben Maimon (better known as Maimonides) noted "the beneficial role that phys-

---

[7]. For an appreciation of sporting and religious values in Montherlant, see MEUNIER, R. (1988). "La conception religieuse du sport chez H. de Montherlant" in *Sports, arts et religions*. G. ANDREU (ed.). Paris, Éditions C. R. Staps: 40-46.

ical exercise plays in stabilizing the various functions of the organism" [TALMUD 2006].

At times, Christianity has shared the reluctance of its forefather in religion. In its most rigorist interpretation (which was only marginally accepted), it came to condemn sports in quite severe terms. In the early 3rd Century, Tertullian (ca. CE 160-225), one of the Fathers of the Church, warned the faithful, "Wherever there is pleasure, there is passion; otherwise the pleasure would be unpleasing. Wherever there is passion, there is jealousy also; otherwise the passion would be unpleasing... You should recognize that it is unwholesome to watch the spectacles in the stadium – for the kicks, the punches, the slaps and the myriad insults which occur there, degrade the majesty of man and the image of God. You will not live better by witnessing senseless races, discus throwing trials, or long jumps that are no less foolish. Do not be fooled into extolling these meaningless and sometimes deadly displays of violence, even less those regimens they demand by which men strive to gain a new body, as if to reform the work of God. No, you should detest these men who are fattened simply to indulge the idleness of the Greeks. Fighting is an invention of the devil." [TERTULLIAN 198: XV and XVIII.].

For his part, St. John Chrysostom (ca. CE 347-407), the 4th Century Bishop of Constantinople who never rested from controversy, referred to the race course of his city as the "Satanodrome" and the games "a devilish procession and satanic spectacle" [KAZHDAN & CONSTABLE 1982: 66].

Closer to our own day, we can recognize these same lingering sentiments when a monk or nun reproves a student for missing a catechism class because of a conflicting sports practice; even though that same religion teacher may be willing to excuse another student who is a musician for missing the same class in order to attend a concert practice.

There are undoubtedly fundamentalists on both sides to condemn the Habs in the name of Catholicism, or Catholicism in the name of the team. (While the second possibility may be more likely than the first, we cannot exclude either.) Generally, the Habs and the Catholic Church have managed to live in harmony for many years. As the two leading institutions of Quebec, they would probably risk too much if they attempted to compete with one another. That may help to explain why, in its press releases, The Habs state that it does not benefit from the religiosity that Quebec culture has lent to it.

Part II
Habs' Passion
On the Thin Red Line between Faith and Idolatry[1]

---

[1] This text comes from a lecture I delivered during "They Hockey Conference. An International Scholarly Conference" at the University of Buffalo, NY, 3-5 May 2010. I want to express my profound gratitude to my wife, Patricia Bauer, both an expert in English and Theology, and to my daughter Marion Bauer both an expert in English and Hockey who have carefully and generously read this paper and corrected my mistakes. Everything, which still remains wrong, the ideas and the way to express them, is my own fault.

Chapter 5
The Habs

A Religion in Quebec

Just remember how the Encyclopædia Britannica defines religion: *"Human beings' relation to that which they regard as holy, sacred, spiritual, or divine. Religion is commonly regarded as consisting of a person's relation to God or to gods or spirits. Worship is probably the most basic element of religion, but moral conduct, right belief, and participation in religious institutions are generally also constituent elements of the religious life as practiced by believers and worshipers and as commanded by religious sages and scriptures"* [ENCYCLOPÆDIA BRITANNICA, n.d.]

According to this definition, do the Habs qualify as a religion?

At the beginning of the first part of this book, I was certainly too quick to conclude "that in a strict sense, the Habs do not comprise a religion" because it "lacks a presumed and explicit reference to something ultimately transcendent – to a Divinity, whatever S/He may be". I should have known that in matter of religion nothing is ever definitive. In fact, there are gods in hockey and worshipping the Habs is a way to deal with them.

Reading Montreal's newspaper, hearing Montreal's radio and watching Quebec's television is enough to convince you that the Habs are a religion, even if you know that religious metaphors are a kind of tank in which journalists dig easily. *"The main chapters of the Book of the Revelation of God* [i.e. The Bible] *are in fact one of the main sources for the vocabulary used by journalists in covering major sporting events."* [BONNETAIN 1991: 15].

- As Polytheism, the Habs have many gods whom you are better to fear: *"The Habs tempted the gods with their sense of entitlement at the start of this landmark season"*[Webster 2009].
- As in Judaism and Christianity, God gives human responsibilities: *"And on the eighth day, Kovy scored."*[STUBBS 2009].
- The saviours are always paradoxical, as Jesus was: *"The goalie is always easiest to blame, and that is Jesus Price's cross to bear."*[BERRA 2009].
- There is a clergy and a liturgical calendar: *"Guy Carbonneau believes Sunday should be a day of rest."*[HICKEY 2009].
- And, as in every religion, there are theologians: *"Decoding the Code could keep a team of Talmudic scholars busy for a week."* [BOONE 2009], *"Every self-anointed hockey expert in town wanted Carbonneau's head on a Platter."* [TODD 2009].

It is a fact. In Quebec, the Habs are not only a hockey team, not only an entertainment business, not only a cultural phenomenon, not only a social fact but also a religion. They really play the role (under certain circumstances and for certain people) of a religion.

a. Hockey's Gods

When Francophone Quebecers commentators describe a hockey game, they all have the same curious habit to give life to the puck. The puck is able to jump, to float, or to deflect all by itself. At the end, the puck can roll in favour of one or the other team.

Even if I do not want to put too much emphasis to this kind of expression (it could just be a cliché or a verbal tic), I want to take it seriously and consider that, for the Francophone commentators at least, the puck lives 'her' (in Quebec French language, "puck" is a feminine word) own life. There are times when she is no longer under the players' control and when she does not follow the basic laws of physic anymore such as gravity and friction. When the puck deflects "by accident" over the board or the window, either she acts by herself or she is handled by the fate or by Hockey's gods. In Montreal, these gods have a name. They are called the Forum's Ghosts, (as for Jesus disciples, there is many different lists of those Forum's Ghost: Georges Vézina is always one of them, as are Newsy Lalonde, Howie Morenz, Hector Toe Blake and Jacques Plante; some lists add Maurice Richard, Patrick Roy and the fourteen other players who made the Habs win their twenty-four Stanley Cups, all won at the Forum, the former mythical Habs' rink, and whose jersey were retired).

But think of what it implies! if the puck is alive or if the puck is under the control of some Superior Being, playing hockey would require more than extra-skilled players with healthy habits, which are a kind of the "moral conduct" required by every religion, more than a wealthy franchise, which is the "religious institution", and more than a generous owner, a wise General Manager and a smart head coach, three species of "religious sages". All those human qualities would be surely needed. But they would not be enough! Such a conception makes sense, because the same team, with the same players and the same coach, with the same equipment in the same rink, can win easily one day and lose poorly the next day. "Glorieuse incertitude du sport", as Francophones say. If Hockey's Gods existed, therefore, winning would also require that the fans believe in their team whatever happens (here is the "right belief"), and that they watch the game (here is the "worship"). But, and that is where the Habs – as any other sports team – become a religion. it would also require that the Habs' fans have this personal "relation to God or to gods or spirits", who could be the puck herself (just think of players or fans carefully keeping pucks of some first or winning goals), the Forum's Ghosts or the God of someone's more traditional religion.

If you consider that the puck is alive or that the puck is under the control of some indefinite Superior Being, you can easily understand coaches', players' and fans' behaviour, their superstitions, their rites, their prayers or their obsessive routine. They try to control the puck, to make her rolling on the "good side", a side, which is always their side, and their beloved team's side. They try to reduce the unexpected, the *Aleas* [CAILLOIS 2001]. They try to win the Superior Being's support, at the same time *fascinans* and *tremendum* as every Holy [OTTO 1958]. As in every rite, they try to give something in order to receive much more, *do-ut-des* principle [VAN DER LEEUW 1986] or Gift-Return Gift system [MAUSS 2000]. They try to ward off bad luck and to be in favour with every Superior Being who could help them.

b. State of Grace

As Jesus was transfigured, as mystics can reach ecstasy, as Buddhists can reach the Nirvana, as Hindus can merge with Siva, players can be in the Zone or in a State of Grace and live moments when and where nothing seems impossible.

Patrick Roy (Saint-Patrick in the Habs' religion) experimented a lot of incredibly powerful moments. But there is one, which is quite different from every other. On April 11 1986, the goaltender was twenty years old and he played his first season with the Habs. He played against the Rangers at the Madison Square Garden, the third game of a Conference final. The game was tied – 1 to 1 – at the end of regulation time. During overtime, the young goalie stopped every single shot and the Habs won 2 to 1. Roy will remember this overtime forever. Twenty-two years later, when his jersey was retired in Montreal, in an interview, he declared: *"To be honest with you, the overtime was the best feeling I ever had. It happened a couple of time. [...] But that night some how I could do whatever I want. I think I could go outside of my net and the guy will shoot on me. I'm just kidding you but I felt so good. I knew there was nothing that was going through."* [ROY 2008]

But the Grace touches not only Habs' goaltenders. Sometimes, it also helps other players. On January 17 2006, the Washington Capitals played against the Phoenix Coyotes. Alexander Ovechkin – Alexander the Great, in NHL mythology – was 21 years old. It is important because Grace loves young players with their innocence. The Russian player got the puck at the centre ice. He went on the right wing, tried to come back to the centre, turned around a Coyotes defenseman. But his opponent resisted. Ovechkin skated behind the net and fell down by himself. He was lying down on his back, the head completely turned on the other side. But he kept the puck. Blindly, with the curve of his stick, he pushed the puck under his back and scored a goal that no human could have ever scored, without the help of Hockey's gods. They surely should have got the assist on this play[1].

It was almost bound to happen that I evoke a goaltender and a top scorer. Not because they got more Grace than a defenseman or than a referee, but because they make this Grace more visible than any other players. And at the end, the association of a goaltender and a top scorer also reminds us that in hockey as in every sport, one's Heaven is always the other's Hell!

c. "Les avoir trempées dans l'eau bénite"

Here is a rather crude Quebec expression. When the Habs won a tough game very luckily, Montrealers say that the players "have had them dipped into the Holy Water". By "them, they do not refer to the players' skates, nor to the players' hands, but to the more private and more masculine parts of the anatomy.

It is crude, but this is very meaningful expression. And it says a lot about the Habs' religion. Obviously, it refers to a traditional Catholic act of piety, consisting of dipping one's fingers into the Holy Water fonts before entering a church, in a process of sanctification and purification. Of course applied to the Habs, it is just a metaphor. Nobody thinks that the players really do what the expression suggests... But it is revealing a very religious, very Christian and quite Catholic way of thinking:

1. There are wins for which players do not deserve all the credit;
2. You can ask for God's help in performing some rituals;
3. Therefore, when the Habs win such an undeserved victory, it is because God was with them;
4. And for God to have helped them, they should have performed the right ritual.

The expression defines the Habs' religion as Catholicism. It catholicizes the God from whom Habs' fans are waiting for help, because he is the only God susceptible to answer to such a catholic behaviour. Obviously, it is not a surprise in a Quebec, which is (or at least was) massively Catholic and is still deeply soaked in a Catholic Culture, whether Quebecer are taking part to the Mass or not.

---

1. You have to see it in order to believe it: Tsoonami. (November 8, 2006). *Ovechkin's incredible goal*. Webpage consulted on 27 November 2008: http://www.youtube.com/watch?v=vzbmI6-YsnQ.

d. Believing against all evidences

I add a last clue of the Habs being a religion. There was a time (from the fifties to the seventies) when the Habs' superiority was not a matter of faith, but just a matter of fact. Any reasonable person had to just acknowledge that the Stanley Cup belonged to Montreal where it was coming back almost every year. But times are changing. Since 1993, the Habs fail, year after year, to win a Stanley Cup. In this period no reasonable person would affirm the Habs being the best team in the NHL. Nobody would affirm it as a fact, but you can just confess it as a deep conviction. The Habs' religion, and it is precisely where it becomes a religion, requires to trust the Habs no matter what, hoping every year that the Cup will return to Montreal. But in a time of Cup shortage, the Habs force the faithful fans to believe against all evidences, despite the poor line up, despite the hurt players, despite the lack of Francophone players, despite the fact that the best players prefers to play for other teams, despite every problem on the ice, in the office, in the medias or outside the rink. A fan has nothing left other than be faithful and just believe.

A mischievous blogger wrote about the Toronto Maple Leafs: *"Cheering for the Leafs is like going to church when you know there's no God."* [SD2SMITH 2008]. He was wrong of course. A true believer cheers for his team whatever the results are, because he hopes there is a God especially in difficult times.

Chapter 6
Making the Habs a Religion

Until now a Habs' religion still remains theoretical. But in Montreal, it is not difficult at all to find some examples of people mixing Habs and religion. I will propose two different ways I called by the name of the person who shared it with me. They are quite different. Victoria uses her Catholic religion in order to make the Habs win. Therefore Victoria way belongs to this inclusive model, where sport is included in one's religion. But Jonathan has made the Habs his own religion. Jonathan way belongs to this syncretic model, where sport and religion are totally confused.

a. The Victoria way

Last year, after having taken part in a program on Radio Ville-Marie (a Christian radio station in Montreal), I got an email from a listener. She wrote to me: *"My daughter Victoria who likes to go to the Bell Centre since we have lived in Montreal (3 years), had given a talk about Frère André on February 19, 2008. She had distributed Frère André's medals and small statue to each of her classmates (what a surprise, her gift made everybody happy). On the same evening, all the family seated with some guests in a suite watching the Habs-Rangers game. You remember. The Habs were crushed, something like 5-0... I suggested to my daughter (she was 11 years old) to ask Frère André for some help. He owed her one with the 'apostolic ad' she made on the same day in her classroom. No sooner said than done and for each prayer, Bing... the Habs were scoring. And it was going on and on in a way that the other guests didn't believe what they were seeing. I shall have confessed them that Victoria was imploring Frère André's help. Without getting ahead of myself, she is the one who quickly gets favours from the Heaven, but she didn't overuse her power (unfortunately). At the end, the whole suite gang was congratulating Frère André. I really had the impression that the Blessed was playing with the team. The Rangers confessed in the newspapers that they didn't understand... 'The puck speeds straight into the net'. We really saw a supernatural intervention, without any bigotry. In the elevators, Victoria was meeting with happy people. And she was telling me: 'You know, it is thanks' to me they are happy, but they do not know... It is rather thanks to Frère André.' On the next day, the medias was talking about a unique game, the game of the century... It just made Victoria prouder and more confident in Frère André. But she keeps secret having made Frère André play with the Habs on this famous February 18, 2008, one year ago."* [Anonymous 2009].

Victoria and her mother believe that Saint Frère-André can help the Habs. They are not alone among the catholic population. On the contrary, in Montreal, the fans piety is deeply bounded to the Catholicism, especially to the Saint-Joseph Oratory, founded by Saint Frère-André, a place of pilgrimage where pilgrims believe they can be cured by touching Saint Frère-André casket, by lighting up some candles in front of Saint-Joseph crypt or by climbing the stairs leading to the Oratory on their knees. The Saint-Joseph Oratory is considered a place for miracles and that's why, when Habs' fans are full of doubts, when they do not believe the Habs can win by themselves, they do not hesitate to go up the mountain in order to ask for some help from Saint Joseph and Frère-André.

On April 14, 2010, one day before the Habs begin the first round of play-offs against the Capitals, a sport Radio organized such a pilgrimage at the Oratory [LAJOIE 2010]. Warned (not divinely, but by one of my students), I decided to take part of it. We were around twenty people, most of them young adults, wearing Habs' jersey (there was two "Maurice Richard", two "Jean Béliveau" and one "Scott Gomez") who performed on a terrace outside a parody of the Catholic mass conducted by the radio animator and then went down into the crypt to light up candles wishing for a win for the Habs.

Figure 5: Lighting up candles for the Habs at the Saint-Joseph Oratory

Of course, we performed the ritual especially for the media. It was more a parody than a real celebration. But parody is a good way to perform something unusual, especially for a big guy wearing hockey jersey. After the media left the chapel, several participants discreetly lighted up their own candle. "I did it so that no one gets hurt", told me one of these worshippers...

b. The Jonathan way

The Jonathan way is quite different. Instead of using his Christian faith, or any other traditional faith, in order to help the Habs, Jonathan (for real or for laugh, it is impossible to decide) made the Habs the object of his religion.

Jonathan, a young adult, PhD student, has a Facebook page entitled "Hockey Temple (of the Canadiens)" [CHA 2008]. He posted 27 pictures of the Habs' Temple he built inside his own apartment.

The Temple consists in a room full of relics and liturgical objects, to the Habs' glory. There are Habs' jerseys, Habs' flags, Habs' pucks, Habs' sticks, Habs' players' bobble heads, red and white candles, etc. In a corner, there is an old Forum's seat, on which Jonathan sits only during the Habs play-off games. But, since a picture is worth a thousand words, here is the most impressive picture, the one entitled "The Procession Alley, a religious and symbolic pregame ritual".

Figure 6: "The Procession Alley, a religious and symbolic pregame ritual"

In the centre of the room, Jonathan built an altar, raised by four steps (one step for each playoff rounds) made of twenty pucks with the Habs' logo, small Habs' figurines, and two candles (one red and one white) on each side. And on the upper step there is a small Stanley Cup, of course. On his Facebook page, he presents a picture of his altar. It is entitled "Oh! My lord Stanley! The altar, the candles, the Holy-Grail and the four steps to climb up before reaching it".

Figure 7: "Oh! My lord Stanley! The altar, the candles, the Holy-Grail and the four steps to climb up before reaching it"

Does Jonathan really believe in the Habs? The question is impossible to decide. But neither on his Facebook page nor in any conversation I had with him, did Jonathan let me think that maybe all that is just a kind of derision.

In fact, I don't think it really matters to know if Jonathan is serious. If we just look at the picture, we clearly see a piety toward the Habs. Jonathan does not give his faith to any God. Jonathan does not believe in any Superior Being he would consider able or ready to help the Habs. Obviously Jonathan trusts the Habs themselves. In Jonathan's religion the Habs are the Gods, the Divinities, the Absolute, the Sacred or the Force, whatever name Jonathan will give to it.

But we have to notice that Jonathan organizes his Habs' religion in a very Catholic way, which one more time is not surprising in a very Catholic Quebec. The Temple quite looks like a traditional Catholic church. There is a central alley that leads to the choir, a lateral chapel, a lot of relics, etc. There is an altar with some sacred vessel on it. Neither are we in a Protestant church, nor a Synagogue, nor a mosque, but in a Catholic church. But at the centre, on the altar, instead of a chalice or a monstrance, there is the Stanley Cup. And on the wall, at the right place where the crucifix would be hanged in a church, there is a Habs' jersey. In fact the Temple is built on such a very traditional catholic pattern, that the altar is against the wall. And therefore, a priest should celebrate the liturgy turning his back to the worshippers.

Chapter 7
Three Dogmas of the Habs' Religion

There is no more doubt that in Montreal, the Habs can be a religion. The Habs not only can be understood as a religion in a theological study, but they can also be lived as a religion by fans/believers in both Victoria and Jonathan ways.

In every religion, there are dogmas or values according to which believers shall live their life. And the Habs' religion makes no exception. It contains different dogmas, it promotes different values and I want to point three of them.

In the first part of this book, I briefly cited Tom Sinclair-Faulkner, who defined the three main values that hockey promotes: *"In the hockey cosmos one is Canadian, one is manly (a quality which goes beyond sheer masculinity), and that one is excellent (by which I mean something that has more to do with winning than with the ancient Greek notion of arete)."* [SINCLAIR-FAULKNER 1977: 391]. Now, I want to analyse more specifically what those values mean for Habs' believers. I will ignore the third one (which is not proper to ice hockey) and substitute it as the third dogma, a value, which belongs only to the Habs. I will consider the first value, formulated in a slightly different way (because in the Habs cosmos, one is Quebecer), for the second dogma. Because the manliness seems so important for every hockey team, every hockey player, every hockey fan, and also for the Habs, I will make it the first dogma.

a. Hockey's dogma: "A man, you shall be!"

I do not ignore how ambiguous it is when hockey players need to prove their virility. Being a man should require no proof! Being a man should be simply a matter of fact. It is always odd (and a little bit disturbing) when a man feels he needs to prove his virility. But I concede that maybe it is normal in hockey, a paradoxical sport where players are wearing at the same time a jockstrap, a cup and a garter belt!

But in hockey one must be manly and this manliness responds to very precise stereotypes. I give two examples of how hockey constructs the kind of virility or manliness it requires: the playoff beard and the Goaltender's Sacrifice.

- The playoff beard is a good way to show on one's own face how successful one's team is. The longer the beard is, the longer the team plays, so the better the team is! But it is also the best way to show one's own virility. Because a beard is the best way to separate men from children which by the way is the goal of the playoff. The playoff beard works as a rite of institution as defined by Pierre Bourdieu, an attempt to transform cultural differences into natural ones. But there is more. Bourdieu noticed that the first function of rite of institution such as circumcision was the most secret one. *"In fact, the most important division, and one which passes unnoticed, is the division it creates between all those who are subject to circumcision, boys and men, children or adult, and those who are not subject of it, i.e. girls and women [...] The most important effect of the rite is the one which attracts least attention: by treating men and women differently, the rite consecrates the difference, institutes it, while at the same time instituting man as man, i.e. circumcised, and woman as woman, i.e. not subject to this ritual operation."*[BOURDIEU 1999: 118]. In this perspective, the true meaning of the playoff beard becomes obvious. Its role is neither to indicate which players are taking part to the playoff, nor to distinguish between younger and older players. Playoff beards exist to institute the difference between those who can, could or could have grown a beard (every single man whether they have hockey skill or not), and those who can not and never can grow it – every single woman whether they have hockey skill or not. The true meaning of the playoff beard is to put more virility into hockey.

- There is another field, less symbolic, where hockey requires virility. Hockey asks for physical courage, it requires players ready to give their own body for the team's good. And, in the hockey's history, the biggest sacrifices were made by the goaltenders. They gave a lot of themselves to meet this expectation, to fulfil what was considered as their duty, especially as long they played bare face. In a totally fascinating book legally entitled *Saving Face* [HYNES & SMITH 2008], Jim Hynes and Gary Smith recall the whole history from January 1, 1918, when the NHL gave permission to goalie to dive on the ice, until April 7, 1974 when Andy Brown was the last goalie to *"defended his team's net bare faced"* [HYNES & SMITH 2008: 94], passing by Jacques Plante who was the first NHL goalie to play with a mask at the Madison Square Garden on November 1, 1959. But it was not without difficulties. *"'I had to show good results to keep the mask,' Plante would say later. But even though he did, Plante still had to put up with teammates, reporters and fans who suggested he was a coward."*[HYNES & SMITH 2008: 50]. Of course, the confusion between manliness and craziness, between experience and scares, between courage and temerity concerns not only the goaltenders. It is not until 1979 that the NHL made the helmet compulsory and the facemask or the shield still remains optional. But times are changing. In 2007 a survey showed that almost half of the NHL players were wearing a shield or a facemask [THE HOCKEY NEWS 2007]. The time has gone when Don Cherry could make, in 2004, a statement, which was true but politically incorrect – *"Only French-Canadian players and Europeans wear visors"* [THE CANADIAN PRESS 2009]. The hockey cosmos took time to admit that manliness is not measurable at the number of scares a player is wearing on his face. May we point that in this process French-Canadian and European players were quicker to understand it and to give a new meaning to the masculinity dogma?

b. Quebec's dogma: "French, you shall speak!"

If the Habs' religion was a Quebecer religion, it has to be similar to Roch Carrier's universe [Carrier 2003], where the children of Saint-Justine were spending the winter in three places, *"the school, the church and the skating-rink"* (this text is written on the Canadian five dollars bill), where children were *"ask[ing] God to help us play as well as Maurice Richard"*, where a young vicar was the referee, where a penalized player needed *"to go to the church and ask God to forgive [him]"*, where a Quebecer child could not stand to wear a Leafs jersey, because they were Anglophone (and probably because they were protestant): *"We were 10, 11 or 12 years old. It was like* La Guerre des tuques *[a French Canadian film about a great snowball war between two groups of youth in Quebec.]. It took place in a working class district of Montreal. It was a confrontation of three against three, street against street, Anglophones against Francophones. They were dressed in the blue of the [Toronto Maple] Leafs, the enemy; we, in the red of Le Canadien. Blue, red, and white: the most beautiful sweater in the history of the sport."* [TRUDEL 2001]. If the Habs' religion was a Quebecer religion, it has to be the religion of a Province where a child coud ask God *"to send, as quickly as possible, moths that would eat up [his] Toronto Maple Leafs Sweater"* [CARRIER 2003: 81]. In Quebec's collective memory or collective unconsciousness, the Habs are due to have the Quebec's religion. In Francophone Quebecers' minds, they shall be Catholics. But the reality is different. Indeed, "facts are stubborn things" and the history does not always correspond to the way people see it. I raise three arguments against the dogma of the French essence of the Habs.

1. In 1909, the *Club Athlétique Canadien* (Habs' first name) was founded by two Anglophone businessmen, Jimmy Gardner, one of the directors of the *Wanderers* (an already well established hockey team in Montreal) and J. Ambrose O'Brien, owner of the Renfrew Millionaires, an existing hockey team in Ontario, in order to increase the game's number, to create more rivalry and more interest for hockey, and to draw new patrons to the hockey games. It was obvious that Tancrède Marsil, a Francophone journalist of *Le Devoir*, accused Ambrose O'Brien to just look for "*collecting, in the East [i.e. Montreal Francophone neighbourhoods] some good dough*"[BONNEAU & HAFSI 1996: 35]. At this time, despite his name, the *Canadien* wasn't the team of the *Canadiens*, a nickname used only for the Francophone Canadians at the beginning of the twentieth century.

2. There never was a time when the Habs were a Francophone team. For the first official game (the second game of the Habs' history), a win 7-3 against the Cobalt in 1910 January, there was already one Anglophone player on the ice. His name was Newsy Lalonde and he came from Cornwall, Ontario [GUAY 1990: 259]. The Habs had never made a priority to recruit Francophone players. They just tried to hire the best players whatever the language they spoke: Howie Morenz for example was born in Mitchell, Ontario. His parents have immigrated from Switzerland. He was protestant and the "*Reverend Doctor Malcolm Campbell, moderator of the General Assembly of the Presbyterian Church of Canada*", celebrated his funerals inside the Forum in March 10, 1937 in front of 50'000 persons [GOYENS, TUROWETZ, & DUGAY 1996: 38].

3. In sport, the colour of the jersey could be symbolic. For example, in English soccer, red is the colour of Catholic teams – as Manchester United or Liverpool – and blue is the colour of protestant teams – like Manchester City and Everton. We can apply this key to the hockey in Canada and remark that the Habs are wearing a red jersey and the Leafs a blue one. It makes sense because the red team comes from a Catholic Province and the blue one from a Protestant Province. But in Canada, symbolism due to colours follows different rules. Blue is the colour of Quebec and red is the colour of Canada. Therefore, can we conclude that the colour of their jersey makes the Habs not a Quebecer team, but a Canadian one? Yes we can, if we compare the Habs and the Nordiques of Quebec City who were wearing a terrific blue jersey with some *fleurs de lys* and were obviously playing the Francophone card, blaming the Habs for being too Canadian. That's maybe why nobody calls the Habs "the Red", but always the *Tricolore*, a nickname which makes more sense, because the Habs' logo really contains three colours, red, white and blue but also a nickname that Francophones find probably more acceptable, since it makes reference to a Francophone entity, France's flag.

But one question remains. If the Habs have been for one hundred years a mixed Francophone and Anglophone team, why are French Quebecers so sure they belong to them? Where does this idea come from, that the Habs are a part of them? It is a conviction they can affirm in very passionate – and sometimes exaggerated – terms. *"The Habs, it is not only a story of hockey. At first, it is the story of the courage, of the sacrifice, of the darkness, of the victory of a French-Canadian people who sometimes looks like a Gauls village. The Habs' history is an inspiration for the French-Canadians who find there the recognition of the value, of the skill, of the determination of a Francophone team who built itself in the heart of the struggle which was tearing apart French and Anglo Canadians."* [GARAND 2009: 6].

Quebec owes this Francophone appropriation of the Habs to one man. His name was Maurice Richard and he proved that Quebecer could be better than any Anglo Canadian. *"You can take one thing for granted: since Maurice Richard in particular, the Montreal Canadians are in a way the national team of Quebec."* [Bérubé 1973: 200]. More interesting, it is due to one event in Maurice Richard's life, the "Maurice Richard riot" on March 18, 1955. *"When Maurice Richard was suspended, every single French Canadian felt punished and angry."* [AQUIN & YANACOPOULO 1972: 128]. Upset by the fact that Maurice Richard had been suspended for the play-offs (he had elbowed a referee during a game), Habs fans (united whatever the language they spoke [MELANÇON 2006: 160]) booed, insulted and then physically aggressed Clarence Campbell, the commissioner of the NHL seated in the Forum to watch a game. The Habs' fans forced the interruption of the game and went on a rampage at first around the Forum and then downtown Montreal. A couple of years later, many Quebecers understood this event as the time they dare to stand up. They considered it as the beginning of their Revolution against an unbearable Anglo domination in Montreal. They read it as the starting point of the Quiet Revolution. They considered it as the Great Awakening of the Quebecer Conscience. *"Some cultural observers have called l'affaire Richard [sic] the flashpoint for Quebec's "Quiet Revolution," manifested in the "masters in our own house" policies of Quebec governments in the 1960s as a response to 200 years of English-Canadian and American domination. The "Quiet Revolution" would change the nature of the continent: from the creation of official Canadian biculturalism, to the not-so-quiet terrorism of the FLQ, to the long and costly battle between Canadian federalists and Quebec indépendantistes to decide what a nation really means."* (MCKINLEY 2000: 189-190). For Maurice Richard and for the Maurice Richard's riot, the Habs will embody this Pride to be a Francophone Quebecer.

c. Habs' dogma: "Through suffering, you shall win!"

I already mentioned it, in the Habs' locker room is written the famous Flanders Fields' verses in the original English words – "To you, from failing hands, we throw / The torch; be yours to hold it high" – and in a French version – *"Nos bras meurtris vous tendent le flambeau, à vous toujours de le porter bien haut*". Chosen during the season 1952-1953 by Dick Irvin [CLUB DE HOCKEY DES CANADIENS DE MONTRÉAL 2008] – or Frank Selke [BRUNEAU & LÉANDRE 2003: 232] –, the verses became the Habs motto. They were scrupulously overwritten in the new Habs' locker room at the Bell Centre.

I do not want to discuss the real effect of this motto on the players. But I want to show the singularities of the French version. It is neither the exact translation of the poem of John McRae, nor the official translation – "*À vous jeunes désabusés, À vous de porter l'oriflamme*" [AU CHAMP D'HONNEUR 1998]. Between the English and the French versions, there are small differences and a lot of meaning lives in these details.

The *"failing hands"* became "bruised arms" ("*bras meurtris*") provoking a triple change: an extension from hands to arms, a passage from a failure to a sufferance and a passage from active voice (the hands are failing) to a passive way – the arms are bruised. From passive to Passion, there is just a small step that we can make, according to the Quebecer context. The passage from "failing hands" to "our bruised arms" (and the possessive pronoun takes all my doubts about the arms' owner) makes sense in the context of a catholic Quebec. It evokes other bruises, those of the crucified Christ, at the centre place of each Catholic Church. And it evokes a very common expression in Quebec: "we are born only for a small bread roll". The Habs' motto corresponds exactly to this dolorist Quebecer mentality. But at the same time, it eludes its marker. Because the Habs let the Quebecers hope for more than a small bread roll, thanks to the Habs, thanks to their successes, Quebecer can hope for and require a big bread, even a brioche, or the whole bakery! With its 24 Stanley Cup, the Habs are the professional hockey team who has won the most Cups and it is the second most successful sports organization just behind the Yankees of New York. But affirming in French that the torch (that probably stands for the ability to win, the pride and the responsibility to continue the tradition) is hold by bruised arms, the Habs recall that it is through a compulsory suffering that Quebecers could win.

Chapter 8
The Habs' Religion is not My Religion

After having exposed as fairly as possible the different arguments that authorize me to speak about a Habs' religion, I can confess that the Habs' religion is not my religion and that the God in the Habs' religion is not a God I want to believe in. I give three reasons why.

1. The Habs' religion is too fragile of a religion. One tends to forget that the Habs have existed for only one hundred years. It is surely a long time for a hockey team. It could be long for anything in North America. However it is very short for a religion. The future of the Habs is not guaranteed, nor is the future of the Habs' religion. Of course, the peculiar status of the Habs (one of "The Original Six", the only French team in the NHL) protect it. But when money is involved, nothing is ever sure. The Habs could be sold and moved to another city. As strange as it can seem in the Quebec today (Quebecers are convinced that Churches will have disappeared long before the Habs), I think that Christianity will last longer than the Habs.

2. The Habs' religion is too tribal of a religion. The Habs' religion is always at risk of monopolizing God. God would be the Habs' God and only the Habs' God. It requires at least to denigrate the other teams the Habs

play against (and not "play with" in this case), too often to hate the cities they belong to and often to insult their fans and sometimes to fight with them. I believe a true religion promotes love, not hate.

3. And the Habs' religion is a too selective of a religion. The Habs are an extremely selective business, a kind of embodiment of the selection. It represents the summit of a pyramidal system, which become smaller and smaller by elimination, as one climb up in the hockey system. But the religion in which I believe is not a selection but an election. God do not award a salary because one deserves it, but it chooses by grace, some will say some person and some people, I will say every person and every people. I know it is unfair. And I know the Habs could not survive with such a model. That's why it is not my religion, what could give sense to my life. I also know that the NHL could seem less selective, taking from to the first teams in order to give back to the last ones, with the draft, and the salary cap. But there is nothing generous in there. The only point is to make the teams more equal for a championship more disputed and more interest form the media and therefore more money. According to me, a religion where the most important is to win (games or money) is a bad religion.

But if the Habs are a bad religion, they are a good hockey team. Even if they are at risk of idolatry, they offer solid opportunities for developing someone's faith, as long as they keep a hockey team.

Chapter 9
On the Thin Red Line between Faith and Idolatry

As Daniel Lys (my former Old Testament professor at the *Institut Protestant de Théologie* in Montpellier, France, back in the eighties) used to say, idolatry has two faces. Obviously, there is idolatry when you worship a false god. But there is also idolatry to worship the true God in a false manner.

Without any doubt, we meet the both forms of idolatry in the Habs religion. To make from a long story a short one, Jonathan worships a false God and Victoria worships the true God but in a false manner.

a. God be with the Habs!

Jonathan has made the Habs the object of his religion. That's the Habs he worships. In the Habs he trusts. That's why Jonathan way is idolatry: it is worshipping a false God. In order to demonstrate it, I need to present a small piece of my own protestant theology.

For me, it is more than knowledge, it is a conviction that God does not reveal himself only on Sunday in a Church but he also can (he never shall, not even in a Church) reveal himself on Friday in a Mosque, on Saturday in a Synagogue, every day in every places and of course on Saturday evening at the Bell Centre. In the same perspective, I believe God does not reveal himself only through pastors, priests, imams and rabbis but he also can (he never shall, not even through a priest) reveal himself through everybody, hockey players included. And I also believe God does not reveal himself only in religious words and music, in liturgical rituals or in sacred objects, but he also can (he never shall, not even in the Bible) reveal himself in every word, every song every rite, every object, including a hockey stick.

I can represent this model in the following diagram:

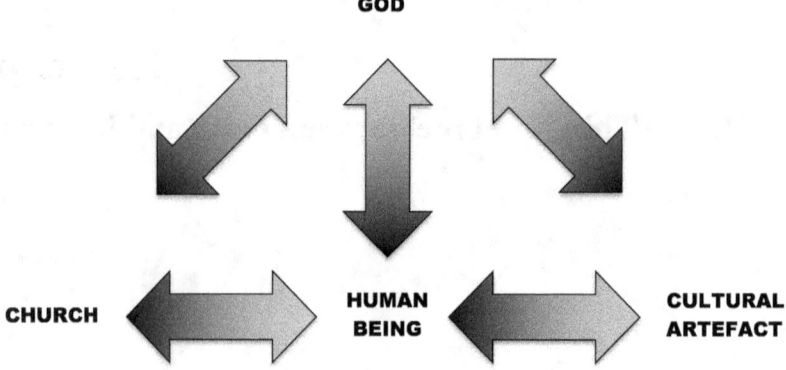

Figure 8: God's Revelation

I add two remarks to make this diagram more understandable:

- The "Church" – any Church – is just one of the possible way God uses to establish relation with human beings. This relation can also be direct or through any cultural artefact – I mean except a Church, because even a Church is a cultural artefact – such as a song, a person, a film, a gesture, etc.
- This conception depends on the double inspiration theory. God, by his Spirit, inspires the person who produces an artefact for it becomes God's Word or God's Picture or God's Gesture, etc. But God also inspires the person who perceives the artefact for it becomes God's Word, Picture, Gesture for him or her.

As every cultural artefact, a beautiful Cammalleri goal, a great Price save or a solid Markov body check are able to carry God's revelation... if the person who looks at them is able to perceive them as a foretaste of the beauty, the perfection, the pleasure who will become real and complete in God's Kingdom. Cammalleri's, Price's or Markov's gestures become God's gesture when they make fans dream of the time when we all will be able to score like Cammalleri, to save like Price and to check like Markov. A Cammalleri goal can transmit God's word for the one who is able to understand it like a sign of the harmony God wants for all of us. A beautiful Cammalleri goal works as a sign of the irruption of God's Kingdom in every day life, as a miracle, which shows the power of God and his loving care for the world and me exactly as he cares for Cammalleri and the Habs.

For me it is clear: a beautiful Cammalleri goal can work as a religious artefact, proper to reveal God to the one who has eyes and knows how to use them. But there is one condition: it requires considering Cammalleri not as a God, but as God's messenger, a kind of angel; it requires making the Habs a part of "the Culture" (included them in the rectangle on the right of the diagram), placing them on the same line as "the Church" as "the Human Being".

The distinction is capital because we are always at risk to give Cammalleri all the credit for the goal, and to consider him as a Superior Being with supernatural powers. And at this time, the player becomes precisely what a theologian would call an idol. Félix Leclerc, for example, succumbs to Félix Leclerc succumbs to this temptation when on October 19, 1983 he wrote a poem for Maurice Richard in which he used messianic terms: "[As for] *Maurice Richard, when he shoots, America screams. When he scores, the deaf hear. When he is punished, telephone lines jump. When he passes, recruits dream. It is the wind that skates. It is all of Quebec standing, inspiring fear in him who lives. It's snowing!*"[PELLERIN 1988: 11]. And of course, that's exactly where the Habs are at risk to become idolatry. *"It is customary in Protestant theology to analyze the performance of a man, his Leistung, as Martin Luther already noted, when speaking of justification by faith. From this perspective, every performance can mutate into either self-justification and idolatry, or human celebration aware of its limitations and relationship to God."* [MÜLLER 2008: 45]. But if we think inside the Christian doctrine of the justification by faith, when we relate it to God, not to a God who pushes the puck himself into the net, but a God who makes Cammalleri able to make outstanding plays, to reach perfection, which will be general in God's Kingdom. Because God's Kingdom is not something which occur after death or after the world's end, but already inside human's life.

That is the whole point and that is why Jonathan is wrong and that is why Jonathan way is idolatry. The Habs can represent an opportunity to meet God, if they are not considered – and of course if they do not consider themselves – as God. It is precisely when fans consider the Habs as a cultural artefact, when they consider players as very skilled Human Beings that the Habs can fulfill a religious function for them and bring God to them and them to God. And maybe the best time to verify if the Habs are a religion or a religious artefact is after a loss. Sports fans love winners. And they worship winning teams! Habs' fans are sure that God is with the Habs when they win – wins proving that God bless the Habs. But how do they deal with defeat? Generally speaking, they think that God has let them down. But they are wrong! They should discover that God is with the Habs also (and maybe especially) in difficult times, when the Habs lost and are eliminated. If they are doubtful, they can remember that Christianity is founded on a defeat, on Jesus' crucifixion. Christians believe that the man who was dying on the cross was the true image of God.

Yes, a beautiful Cammalleri goal is a foretaste of God's Kingdom, because common things – in fact even a lucky goal, even a garbage goal are a foretaste of God's Kingdom but a beautiful goal prevents the blaming of the goaltender – can talk about God's Kingdom, can serve as a parable or as a metaphor of this ultimate reality. A Cammalleri goal could be the theme of a new parable of God's Kingdom. Here is how it begins: "God's Kingdom is like a beautiful Cammalleri goal. The fan who taped it, invited his friend to look at it and look at it again…"

b. God love the Habs!

Victoria way embodies the second form of idolatry, which is worshipping the true God in a false manner. Victoria does not make the same mistake as Jonathan. She does not worship the Habs as a God but she asks God to help the Habs. Nevertheless, Victoria way is a form of idolatry. One more time, I can prove it by presenting another small piece of my own protestant theology.

I do not have any problem (even as a western academic protestant theologian) to affirm that God cares about the Habs, and can intervene into the Habs' life, during Habs' games. God can help General Manager to manage the club, players to play, fans to cheer, team's doctors to cure, technical staff to prepare ice and equipments. I do not have any reason to think that any part of the world or any aspect of the life could be out of God's interest and action. Some believers could qualify as futile to think that God could be interested in the Habs. I do admit there are more important things in the world but it does not mean that God can't be interested in the Habs. I give three reasons why.

1. Even if a Habs win or lose does not change the face of the world, it could have a big impact. Just think at the stakes around the Habs: the money they produce, the jobs they create; and also consider the job's insecurity for some players, the injuries, the dreams it inspires for young players, the pride of the fans. For all that reason, the Habs need a little help from God.
2. God's interest for the Habs does not deprive some other people from more useful, more urgent or more crucial help from God. The God in who I believe is multitasking or omnipotent in more traditional words. He is able to intervene at the same time and with the same efficiency inside the Bell Centre and inside the Madison Square Garden and in any hospital or on any battlefields. And by the way, God has exactly the same interest for every other NHL's teams. Regardless of what could Habs' fans think – and they are very exclusive and very tough on other teams – God blesses the Leafs, the Bruins and the Canucks the same as the Habs. God has a seat at the Air Canada Centre and at the Rexall Place exactly as he has a seat at the Bell Centre. And at the Bell Centre, he helps the Habs exactly as he helps their opponent.

3. I refuse to decide by myself what God should be interested in, what he should care for. I'm not able to put a limit on God's action. What is important enough for God to take care of? What is too futile for God to be interested in? I prefer to let God decides, even if, for my part, I answer: "everything is important enough" at the first question and "nothing is too futile" at the second one.

But I still need to be more specific about the form of God's help for the Habs.

Let us imagine, in a fatalist way, that everything that happens to the Habs (good things like bad things) would depend on God. Such a belief in a direct intervention of God in every aspects of the Habs life would force me to thank him when a player is hurt, when a Habs' player hurts another player. I should consider those facts (they are obviously bad things) as a punishment for bad behaviour (for example a weak game or a lack of will) or as an attempt to balance the game when a team is too strong, or a way to make space for a healthy scratch or a younger player. I know that God works sometimes in mysterious ways, but here it will really be too bizarre.

Neither can I believe that God could deflect a shot, which otherwise would have gone directly in an empty net. In this case, my culture and my faith would make me eliminate all supernatural causes (like a divine or devilish intervention) and I prefer a natural explanation to explain such an accident, like a defect in the ice. In some less obvious moment, when a shot goes off the post for example, I would attribute such an accident to the blunder or the misfortune.

But, I would not conclude that God does not play any role in a Habs' game. I will rather believe (on and off the ice) in the possibility of an indirect intervention of God through people making his will. The French writer Georges Bernanos wrote "God doesn't have any hands but ours". As him, I would confess: "God does not have any hands to control or block the puck but he can inspire player's hands"; "God does not have any brain to invent hockey systems, but he can inspire a coach's mind"; "God does not have any voice to cheer for the Habs, but he can use the fans' voices".

I believe God helps the players who ask for his help. And I concur with the testimony of Daniel Bouchard (a former born again goaltender of the Nordiques of Quebec City) whose nickname was "God's hand". In 1982, he declared, right after a winning game: *"I praise God because he makes stops for me. I was feeling like his tool. I had prayed a lot. Sometimes, it does not get in."* [DESROSIERS & THIBAULT 2009]. Affirming, *"God makes stop for me"* could let us think that Bouchard believes that God was the one who directly intervenes in front of the net. But, being more specific, the goaltender added something very important: *"I was feeling like [God's] hand"*. Now everything becomes clear. God didn't stop the puck by himself. Having no hands, he needed a human hand in order to block the puck. This night, God's hand was Bouchard's left hand. This night, God used Bouchard's hand as his tool

God can help any hockey team, including the Habs. But he never jumps on the ice. He always acts indirectly. He helps the Habs by inspiring General Managers, players and fans rather than moving directly the puck. It is not God who makes the puck bump, jump, deflect or roll for one team or another. It is not God who acts, but he is the one who inspires the player who handle the puck, the people who made the stick and the puck, and the person who cleaned the ice.

Now I can come back to Victoria way and explain why it is idolatry. I wrote that it was a false way to worship the true God. But asking for Frère-André's help could belong to the first form of idolatry. If it means worshipping Frère-André, Victoria would certainly be worshipping a false God. But maybe she is not. Maybe Victoria knows that all Frère-André's powers are coming from God. Maybe she understands that asking for Frère-André's help is asking for God's help. So I hope, even if she didn't mention God once in her email but Frère-André eight times. I can't refrain from thinking that she would be better to ask for God's help directly. It will be the best way to prevent this first form of idolatry, even if it would not atomically prevent the second form of idolatry. But Victoria way is idolatry in its first form first. Victoria way is wrong because it implies that a divine intervention could be automatic or compulsory, under the condition you have the right amount of faith (Victoria *"is the one who quickly gets some favours form the Heaven"*) you accomplish the right acts (Victoria *"had distributed Frère André's medals and small statue to each of her classmates"*), or you perform the right ritual (Victoria's mother *"suggested to [her] daughter to ask Frère André for some help"*). Even if Victoria was worshipping the true God (and I still remain doubtful), Victoria way remains idolatry because it is a false way to worship him. God's intervention can neither be automatic nor compulsory. It always remains God's free decision and no one's piety, as deep as it could be, can change the course of a game or a season. Victoria should better have been praying for the players in order to accept themselves as God's tool.

Afterword

A Fish in the Logo

It is time to conclude and I want to do it by a short meditation. It is called "The fish in the logo" and it looks like a child's game. I could entitle it: "Please, help Olivier to find the blue fish in the Habs' logo!"[1]?

---

[1] This logo is the most recent version of the Habs' logo. It was adopted in 1952. The former versions didn't contain any fish. Club de Hockey des Canadiens. (n.d.). *Les chandails et logo*. Webpage consulted on 23 June 2009: http://notrehistoire.canadiens.com/jerseys-and-logos/1938-2008

Figure 9: The Habs' Logo

Take a few seconds to look at the logo in order to find the fish. I assure you it is here, swimming somewhere in the heart of the picture. In order to make it visible, just take off the big red letter "C", erase both small blue squares and complete the inside blue line. Can you see it now? Once you saw it, it becomes obvious, isn't it?

Everyone knows what the sign of the fish means. Especially in the United States where you can see it on every other car. No doubt, it is a Christian symbol; even one of the first Christian symbols in the world's history, a symbol used long before the cross, already drawn in the catacombs. The fish was – and still is – a Christian symbol because the Greek name of "fish" – *Ictus* – is an acrostic. It compiles to I.C.T.U.S, the Greek letters which stands for Jesus Christ, God's Son and Savoir.

In the first centuries of the Common Era, the fish – the name and the picture – was used as a secret code among Christians. A secret code, because Christians were persecuted. They needed to recognize themselves without being recognized by their enemies. But little by little, Christians tended to prefer the cross to the fish. The symbol of the cross was more evident and its evidence was not a problem once Christianity became the official religion of the Roman Empire. The sign of the fish almost disappeared among Christianity, until the beginning of the twentieth century when Evangelical Christians literally resurrected it, by choosing it as the sign of their faith.

But what about the fish inside the Habs' logo? Is it a subliminal declaration of faith? Is it the proof that the Habs are Christian? With their logo, do the Habs confess their faith? Of course, I do not think so. But, remember the double inspiration theory. Even if the fish in the logo is accidental, or even if the fish in the logo does not have any Christian signification, it does not matter.

I see the fish in the Habs logo. For me it has a Christian value. For me it has the status of a confession of faith. For you too now, I hope. Now, you will not be able to look at this logo the same way any more. Every time you will look at the Habs' logo, you will see the blue fish and remember that Jesus is Christ, God's Son and Saviour.

That is a good way to put some faith, not religion, inside the Habs.

Bibliography

1. Books

Augustine. *De vera religion*, Translated and edited by J. Pegon (1951). Paris: Desclée De Brouwer / Études Augustiniennes: tome 8.

Bauer, O., & Barreau, J.-M. (2009). *La religion du Canadien de Montréal*. Montréal: Fides.

Black, F. (1997). *Habitants et Glorieux: Les Canadiens de 1909 à 1960*. Laval, Mille Îles.

Bonneau, L., & Hafsi, T. (1996). *Sam Pollock et le Canadien de Montréal*. Québec: Presses de l'Université du Québec.

Bonnetain, P. (1991). *Dieu dans le stade*. Lausanne & Levallois-Perret: L'Aire & Manya.

Bourdieu, P. (1999). *Language and Symbolic Power*. Harvard: Harvard University Press.

Bruneau, P., & Léandre, N. (2003). *La glorieuse histoire des Canadiens*. Montréal: Les Éditions de l'Homme.

Caillois, R. (2001). *Man, Play and Games*. Chicago: University of Illinois Press.

Carrier, R. (2003). *The Hockey Sweater*. Toronto: House of Anansi Press Limited.

Cicero. *De natura deorum,* Translated and edited by H. Rackham (1923). Loeb Classical Library.Cambridge, Harvard University Press.
Evans, C. H. et William R. Herzog II (eds) (2002). *The Faith of 50 Million: Baseball, Religion and American Culture.* Louisville, Westminster John Knox Press.
Freud, S. (1999). *L'avenir d'une illusion.* Paris, Presses Universitaires de France.
Gounelle, A. et B. Reymond (2005). *En chemin avec Paul Tillich.* Münster, Lit Verlag.
Goyens, C., Turowetz, A., & Dugay, J.-L. (1996). *The Montreal Forum. Forever Proud.* Westmount: Effix.
Guay, D. (1990). *L'histoire du Hockey au Québec. Origine et développement d'un phénomène culturel.* Montréal: Éditions JCL.
Haldas, G. (1989). *La légende du football.* Lausanne, L'Âge d'Homme.
Hall, D. E., ed. (1994). *Muscular Christianity: Embodying the Victorian Age.* Cambridge, Cambridge University Press.
Hynes, J., & Smith, G. (2008). *Saving Face. The Art and History of the Goalie Mask.* Mississauga: Wiley.
Kazhdan, A. P., & Constable, G. (1982). *People and Power in Byzantium: An Introduction to Modern Byzantine Studies.* Dumbarton Oaks Research Library and Collection.
Lactance. *Institutions divines.* Translated and edited by P. Pierre Monnat (1986). Sources Chrétiennes. Paris, Cerf.
Lévi-Strauss, Cl. (1950). *Mythologiques: Le cru et le cuit.* Paris, Plon.
Luckman, T. (1967). *The Invisible Religion: The Problem of Religion in Modern Society.* New York, Macmillan.
Marx, K. (1843) "Contribution à la critique de la philosophie du droit de Hegel". Webpage consulted on 2 June 2008: http://marx.engels.free.fr/marx/txt/1843critiqueh.htm#bknote1.
Mauss, M. (2000). *The Gift: The Form and Reason for Exchange in Archaic Societies.* New York: W. W. Norton & Company.
McKinley, M. (2000). *Putting a Roof on Winter.* Vancouver : Greystoke Books.
McKinley, M. (2001). *Un toit pour le hockey.* Montréal: Hurtubise.
Melançon, B. (2006). *Les yeux de Maurice Richard. Une histoire culturelle.* Montréal: Fides.
Ménard, G. (2006). *Petit traité de la vraie religion.* Paris, Téraèdre.
Montherlant, H. de (1954). *Les Olympiques.* Paris, Gallimard.
Müller, D. (2008). *Le football, ses dieux et ses démons. Menaces et atouts d'un jeu déréglé.* Genève: Labor et Fides.
O'Brien, A. (1967). *Fire Wagon Hockey.* Chicago, Follett, vi.
Otto, R. (1958). *The Idea of the Holy.* Oxford: Oxford University Press.
Pellerin, J.-M. (1988). *Maurice Richard: l'idole d'un peuple.* Montréal: Éditions de l'Homme.

Pike, K. L. (1954-1960). *Language in Relation to a Unified Theory of the Structure of Human Behavior*. Glendale, Summer Institute of Linguistics.
Putney, C. (2001). *Muscular Christianity: Manhood and Sports in Protestant America, 1880-1920*. Cambridge, Harvard University Press.
Tertullian (198) *Contre les spectacles*. Webpage consulted on 16 June 2008: http://www.clerus.org/clerus/dati/2004-05/26-6/TERTU_14.html.
Traduction œcuménique de la Bible (1982). Paris: Alliance Biblique Universelle & Le Cerf.
Van der Leeuw, G. (1986). *Religion in Essence and Manifestation*. Princeton: Princeton University Press.
Turner V. W. (1972). *Les tambours d'afflication*. Paris, Gallimard.

2. Articles, Booksections

Aquin, H., & Yanacopoulo, A. (1972). "Éléments pour une phénoménologie du sport." In P. Pagé, & R. Legris (eds), *Problèmes d'analyse symbolique*. (pp. 115-146). Québec: Presses de l'Université du Québec.
Bailey, E. I. (1996). "La religion implicite et son réseau d'études: Introduction et présentation." *Religiologiques* (14): 15-35.
Basset, J.-C. et P. Gisel (1995). "Religion et religions." in *Encyclopédie du protestantisme* (pp. 1295-1317). P. Gisel (ed.). Genève, Labor et Fides.
Bauer, O. (2007). "Vers une communauté d'individus. Le cas de l'Église protestante francophone de Washington, DC." in M. Dumais & J. Richard (eds), *Église et communauté* (pp. 59-78). Montreal: Fides.
Bauer, O. (2009). "Introduction." In O. Bauer, & J.-M. Barreau (eds), *La religion du Canadien de Montréal* (pp. 7-18). Montréal: Fides.
Bauer, O. (2009). "Le Canadien est-il une religion?" In O. Bauer, & J.-M. Barreau (eds), *La religion du Canadien de Montréal* (pp. 29-80). Montréal: Fides.
Bellah, R. N. (1967). "Civil Religion in America." *Daedalus* (96): 1-21.
Bérubé, R. (1973). "Les Québécois, le hockey et le Graal". *Voix et images , 7* (1): 191-202.
Bromberger, C., A. Hayot & Mariottini, J.-M.. (1987). "Allez l'O.M.! Forza Juve!" *Terrain* (8): 8-41.
Campiche, R. (1995). "Religion civile." *Encyclopédie du protestantisme*. (p. 1318). P. Gisel (ed.). Genève, Labor et Fides.
Chanson, P. (2001). "Syncrétisme." in *Dictionnaire œcuménique de missiologie. Cent mots pour la mission*. (329-334). I. Bria, P. Chanson, J. Gadille & M. Spindler (eds). Genève, Labor et Fides:.
Émond, B. (1973). "Essai d'interprétation religieuse du hockey." *Brèches* (1): 80-89.

Encyclopædia Britannica (n.d.) "Religion". Encyclopædia *Britannica Online*. Webpage consulted on 1st April 2008: http://search.eb.com/eb/article-9063138.

Evans, C. H. (2002a). "Baseball as Civil Religion: The Genesis of an American Creation Story." in *The Faith of 50 Million: Baseball, Religion and American Culture*. (pp. 14-33). Christopher H. Evans & William R. Herzog II (eds). Louisville, Westminster John Knox Press.

Evans, C. H. (2002b). "The Kingdom of Baseball in America. The Chronicle of an American Theology." in *The Faith of 50 Million. Baseball, Religion and American Culture*. (pp. 35-48). Christopher H. Evans & William R. Herzog II (eds). Louisville, Westminster John Knox Press.

Flipo, J.-P. (2003). "L'Église: une organisation comme une autre ?" in *Les Églises au risque de la visibilité*. (pp. XXX). O. Bauer & F. Moser (eds). Lausanne, Institut romand de pastorale 3.

Garand, M.-È. (2009, 16 January). "Le Canadien de Montréal est-il une religion ou la religion des Canadiens?" *Colloque "La religion du Canadien"*. Université de Montréal: 16 janvier 2009.

Garassino, R. (1992). "Les demi-dieux du stade." in *Le corps surnaturé. Les sports entre science et conscience*. (pp. 63-75). C. Genzling (ed.). Paris, Autrement. Sciences en société:.

Jaenen C. (1985). "Amerindian Responses to French Missionary Intrusion, 1611-1760: A Categorization". *Thèmes Canadiens / Canadian Issues* 7: 182-197.

James, W. C. (1999). "Dimorphs and cobblers: Ways of being religious in Canada." *Studies in Religion / Sciences Religieuses* 28 (3): 275-291.

Kerrigan, M. P. (1992). "Sports and the Christian Life: Reflection on Pope John Paul II Theology of Sports." in *Sport and Religion*. (pp. 253-259). S. J. Hoffman (ed.). Champaign, Human Kinetics Books.

Meunier, R. (1988). "La conception religieuse du sport chez H. De Montherlant" in *Sports, arts et religions*. (pp. 40-46). G. Andreu (ed.). Paris, Éditions C. R. Staps .

Maître, J. (2007). "Religion - la religion populaire." in *Encyclopædia Universalis*. Paris.

McKim, D. K. (2002). "'Matty' and 'Ol' Pete': Divergent American Heroes." in *The Faith of 50 Million: Baseball, Religion and American Culture*. (pp. 51-81). Christopher H. Evans & William R. Herzog II (eds). Louisville, Westminster John Knox Press.

Müller, D. (2004). "Le football comme religion populaire et comme culture mondialisée: brèves notations en vue d'une interprétation critique d'une quasi-religion contemporaine." in *Théologie et Culture. Hommage à Jean Richard*. (pp. 299-314). M. Dumas, F. Nault et L. Pelletier (eds). Québec, Presses de l'Université de Laval.

Sabatucci, D. (2007). "Syncrétisme." in *Encyclopædia Universalis*. Paris.

Sinclair-Faulkner, T. (1977). "A Puckish Reflection on Religion in Canada." in *Religion and Culture in Canada*. (383-405). P. Slater (ed.). Waterloo, Wilfrid Laurier University Press:.

Talmud, J. (2006). "La formation médicale de Maïmonide et son actualité au regard de l'activité physique et de la santé." *Histoire des sciences médicales* 40 (1): 73-82.

Tertullian (198) *Contre les spectacles*. Webpage consulted on 16 June 2008: http://www.clerus.org/clerus/dati/2004-05/26-6/TERTU_14.html

Trudel, P. (2001). "Préface" in *Un toit pour le hockey*. M. McKinley. Montréal: Hurtubise.

3. Medias

Barnard, A. (2010). "Imam Says He's Open to Options on Islamic Center," *The New York Times*, 14 September 2010, A22.

Berra, L. (2009, 16 January). *The Loneliest Man in Sports*. Webpage consulted on 14 April 2009: http://sports.espn.go.com/espnmag/story?section=magazine&id=3836512

Boone, M. (2009, 27 February). *The Code carries a message about fighting*. Webpage consulted on 14 April 2009: http://www.montrealgazette.com/story_print.html?id=1334058&sponsor=

Desrosiers, P., & Thibault, S. (2009, February). *Les Francs-Tireurs*. Épisode #286. TéléQuébec.

Gervais, L.-M. (2008, 14 October). "L'entrevue – Le Canadien, objet d'étude en théologie." Le Devoir. Webpage consulted on 20 October 2008: http://www.ledevoir.com/sports/hockey/210532/l-entrevue-le-canadien-objet-d-etude-en-theologie

Hickey, P. (2009, 9 February). "Struggling Habs take act on the road." *The Gazette*.

Lajoie, J.-C. (2010, 14 April). "Jean-Charles en pélerinage pro-CH à l'Oratoire St-Joseph." *CKAC Sports*.

Stubbs, D. (2009, 22 February). "And on the eighth day, Kovy scored." *The Gazette*.

The Canadian Press. (2009, 5 February). *Still loud and proud, hockey broadcaster Don Cherry turns 75*. Webpage consulted on 7 May 2009: http://thehockeynews.com/articles/23151-Still-loud-and-proud-hockey-broadcaster-Don-Cherry-turns-75.html.

The Hockey News. (2007, 26 October). *Visor use still rising in NHL*. Webpage consulted on 7 May 2009: http://www.theglobeandmail.com/servlet/story/RTGAM.20071026.wsptvisors26/GSStory/GlobeSportsHockey/.

Todd, J. (2009, 16 March). "Carbo went from toast to roast." *The Gazette*, B1.

Valentine, H. (2002), "The Emperor's Derrière: The Changed Vision of Quebec Independence," *Le Québec Libre*, No. 104 (Montreal, May 11, 2002), 1.
Webster, N. (2009, 15 March). "Canadiens pay for Hubris." *The Gazette*, A1.

4. Internet

"La Bataille Générale Canadiens – Nordiques du Vendredi Saint."(1984). Webpage consulted on 2 June 2003: http://www.youtube.com/watch?v=hqsVXIhwAzA.

"Maradona - Hand of God Goal." (2006, 15 January). Webpage consulted on 29 November 2007: http://video.google.com/videoplay?docid=5642299644828093290.

"Pierre de Coubertin." (2008). Webpage consulted on 16 June 2008: http://www.olympic.org/fr/passion/museum/permanent/coubertin/index_fr.asp

"Canadiens.com." (2008). Webpage consulted on 2 June 2008: http://canadiens.nhl.com/fr/index.html.

Anonymous. (2009, 25 February). *Personal Email*. Montréal.

Au champ d'honneur. (1998, 16 September). Webpage consulted on 30 October 2008: http://www.vac-acc.gc.ca/remembers_f/sub.cfm?source=history/firstwar/vimy/vimy1a

Bélanger, C. (2006). "Events, Issues and Concepts of Quebec History: The Quiet Revolution". Webpage consulted on 10 August 2010: http://faculty.marianopolis.edu/c.belanger/quebechistory/events/quiet.htm

Cha, J. (2008, 6 April). *Le temple du hockey (des Canadiens)*. Webpage consulted on 4 May 2009: http://www.facebook.com

Chabot, J.-F. (2003). "Le match le plus sombre de l'histoire." Webpage consulté on 2 June 2008: http://www.radio-canada.ca/Sportsv1/matchsdesanciens nouvelles/200304/09/001-VendrediSaint.asp

Club de Hockey des Canadiens de Montréal. (2008). *Photo interactive de 360° - Vestiaire du Tricolore*. Webpage consulted on 28 October 2008: http://canadiens.nhl.com/team/app/l_fr?service=page-&page=NHLPage&bcid=fre_int_vestiaire

Club de Hockey des Canadiens de Montréal. (n.d.). *Les chandails et logo*. Webpage consulted on 23 June 2009: http://notrehistoire.canadiens.com/jerseys-and-logos/1938-2008

Philadelphia Flyers. (2008). "Reserve your Playoff Tickets!" Webpage consulted on 15 April 2008: http://flyers.nhl.com/.

Roy, P. (2008, 22 November). "NHL-1 on 1 with Patrick Roy." R. Ferraro, Interviewer. TSN. Webpage consulted on 23 May 2010: http://watch.tsn.ca/nhl/clip113824#clip113824

sd2smith. (2008, 3 December). *Worshipping les Canadiens: story comments*. Webpage consulted on 7 May 2009: http://www.cbc.ca/sports/hockey/story/2008/12/01/montreal-hundredth-religion.html#socialcomment

Tsoonami. (2006, 8 November). *Ovechkin's incredible goal*. Webpage consulted on 27 November 2008: YouTube: http://www.youtube.com/watch?v=vzbmI6-YsnQ.

Author Bionote

Olivier Bauer was born in 1964 in Neuchâtel (Switzerland). He spent his professional life in Practical Theology on three continents, between Protestant Churches and Faculties of Theology. He studied Theology in Neuchâtel, Montpellier and Lausanne where he got his PhD in 2000. He worked for Reformed Churches in France and Switzerland, as a chaplain in a Protestant high school and college in Tahiti (1993-1999) and as pastor of the French speaking Protestant Church of Washington, DC (2003-2006). He has taught theology at the Universities of Lausanne and Neuchâtel and since 2005, and he is professor at the Faculty of Theology and Religious Studies of the University of Montreal. His main academic interests include: the transmission of faith to the five senses; the cultural dimension of Christianity not only abroad but also in Western countries; food and religion. Prof Bauer wrote five books: Le protestantisme et ses cultes désertés (Labor et Fides, 2008); Les rites protestants en Polynésie française (L'Harmattan, 2003); Le protestantisme à table (Labor et Fides, 2000); Petit lexique du parler local (Aux vents des îles, 1999); Le jeu de Dieu et de Jonas (Éditions du Moulin, 1996). He co-edited three books: with Jean-Marc Barreau, La religion du Canadien de Montréal (Fides, 2009); with Prof Félix Moser, Les Églises au risque de la visibilité (IRP, 2002); with Prof Henry Mottu, Le culte protestant (IRP, 2001).

www.ingramcontent.com/pod-product-compliance
Lightning Source LLC
Chambersburg PA
CBHW051408290426
44108CB00015B/2199